SUCCESS
IN THE
LITERACY
HOUR

edited by
Dorothy Smith

A NASEN Publication

Published in 2000

ISBN 1 901485 24 2

Published by NASEN.
NASEN is a registered charity. Charity No. 1007023.
NASEN is a company limited by guarantee, registered in England and Wales.
Company No. 2674379.

Further copies of this book and details of NASEN's many other publications may be obtained from the NASEN Bookshop at its registered office:
NASEN House, 4/5, Amber Business Village, Amber Close, Amington, Tamworth, Staffs., B77 4RP.
Tel: 01827 311500 Fax: 01827 313005 email: welcome@nasen.org.uk
Website: www.nasen.org.uk

Copy editing by Nicola von Schreiber.
Cover design by Raphael Creative Design.
Typeset by J. C. Typesetting.
Typeset in Times and printed in the United Kingdom by Stowes (Stoke-on-Trent).

SUCCESS IN THE LITERACY HOUR

Contents

Acknowledgements

The Editor and publishers wish to extend their grateful thanks to:

- Dr Beryl Smith, of BILD (British Institute of Learning Disabilities), for giving permission for the article *A Multi-Modal Approach to Literacy* by Professor Barry Carpenter to be reproduced. This was first published in *The SLD Experience*;
- the SLD schools (Kent) Literacy Consortium for giving permission for The Literacy Profile to be reproduced;
- Staffordshire County Council Pupil and Student Services for giving permission for the article *The Literacy Hour: Pupils with Hearing Impairment* to be reproduced;
- Harper Perennial for giving permission for the extract from Lee Canter's *Homework without tears* to be reproduced;
- members of NASEN Branches who responded to our appeal for information about their schools' arrangements for the Literacy Hour;
- members of the Publications Sub-Committee for their advice and support, especially Mike Hinson, Tessa Knott and Alec Williams.

Foreword

Early in 1999 the NASEN Publications Sub-Committee published its first contribution to the work in schools concerning the *National Literacy Strategy*. We called the book *Surviving the Literacy Hour* in order to attempt to reflect the feelings of those classroom practitioners who were working with new guidelines and who were being faced with day-by-day organisational problems.

The book contained articles from practising teachers and other educationists and their views were varied. However, these were mostly positive and it seemed that the Literacy Hour was being welcomed by both teachers in mainstream primary and in special schools even though it was in its infancy.

Since *Surviving the Literacy Hour* was published schools have had a full year to work on the Literacy Hour, to reflect on its strengths and weaknesses and to organise it to suit their particular circumstances. Some, who were in the pilot year, have had two years. It has been reported that even after this short time pupils have benefited and their literacy attainments at the end of Key Stage 2 have improved. Summer schools have been set up for pupils at borderline Level 4 in the Key Stage 2 SATs and these also seem to have proved beneficial. In September 1999 secondary schools also took part in the Hour with their Year 7 pupils.

This new book, *Success in the Literacy Hour*, is the more 'substantial handbook' promised in the foreword of *Surviving the Literacy Hour.* It complements the earlier book and takes suggestions and ideas forward. Despite a few reservations most contributors are extremely positive about the Strategy and how beneficial it can be for children with special educational needs. Schools are very different and what works in one school and in one area may not work in another, but readers should be able to take many helpful ideas back to their own schools and to include them in their own teaching practices.

As with the first book, *Surviving the Literacy Hour*, members of NASEN were invited to contribute to this publication but this time it was after they had worked on the Literacy Hour for a year. The same questionnaire as for the previous book was supplied. Respondents were encouraged to describe successes, achievements or failures, to detail tips and pointers or snags and difficulties, to outline organisational arrangements and to give information about programmes of work. Replies arrived from all areas of the country and were from both mainstream schools and special schools. Although Scotland hasn't an equivalent literacy hour it was pleasing to receive contributions from Scottish schools describing their structured reading and writing arrangements. This time the majority of respondents gave both their own names and their school names which are acknowledged at the end of the book.

There have been substantial contributions from teachers in special schools and as well as these forming a forum of good practice to share with similar learning establishments they contain much that should be useful to their mainstream colleagues. With more pupils with quite complex needs entering the mainstream sector teachers will be looking towards the special schools for help, information and guidance.

Success in the Literacy Hour's title has been chosen to reflect the positive feelings felt by the contributors. It is possible that teachers who have not felt so assured by the Literacy Hour did not send any comments. If this is so then it is hoped that they will read *Success in the Literacy Hour* and become more enthusiastic and confident. Pupils with special educational needs deserve the best of teaching. Their teachers are dedicated to making sure that these pupils do not become second class. Despite the lack of real guidance given by the DfEE about managing the Literacy Hour for pupils with special educational needs, teachers have risen to the occasion and have worked out ideas for themselves. *Success in the Literacy Hour* contains a rich source of ideas.

The book falls neatly into three areas: special schools, mainstream primary and secondary schools and contributions from those who work outside schools but who support them. There are articles describing schools' Literacy Hour arrangements, articles from practitioners about their own experiences, articles which are based on research projects, some general 'tips' for teachers and, as in the previous book, compilations from the broad questionnaires returned from class teachers in all sectors of mainstream and special schools. For readers of the previous book George has come out from under the table and has learnt to read. The final article describes data from a DfEE-funded project to examine access to the Literacy Hour of pupils with special educational needs. It is optimistic in its conclusion showing that the Literacy Hour 'has had a major positive impact on literacy teaching in primary schools' and that it has 'generated feelings of success and enthusiasm on the part of both teachers and pupils'. The authors reinforce the fact that schools need to feel confident in modifying the Framework to meet the needs of those children with special educational needs and the contributions from practitioners for *Success in the Literacy Hour* show that when this occurs such children are helped to access the Hour successfully.

Success in the Literacy Hour begins with a poem from Kate Farminer who eloquently describes how individual pupils might cope with the Literacy Hour. One would hope that the 'Tommies' in our classrooms will become well-provided for and that we, as teachers, educators and supporters, learn how to make them happy and able to access the reading and writing skills which they so desperately need.

Dorothy Smith

Contributors

Nick Andrews (Head of Unit) and **Anita Lundy-Overton** (Literacy Co-ordinator), Aspen Unit, Whitfield County Primary School, Dover, Kent.

E. Bentley, J. Harris and **I. Robinson**, members of NASEN, Northants Branch.

Veronica Birkett, Special Educational Needs Consultant, Trainer and Practitioner, Walsall, West Midlands.

David Braybrook, Director of Education, I CAN.

Linda Care, Treetops School, Grays, Essex.

Professor Barry Carpenter, Chief Executive, Sunfield School, Clent, Stourbridge, Worcestershire.

Gill Carter, Freelance OfSTED Inspector.

Anne Dutton, Primary Support Teacher.

Kate Farminer, Teacher, Gloucester.

Malcolm Garner, Service for Hearing Impaired, Visually Impaired and Physically Disabled, Stafford.

A. Holdsworth, Secondary Literacy/English Co-ordinator, Tor View School, Rossendale, Lancashire.

Elaine Holland, Class Teacher and Literacy Co-ordinator, Merstone School, Marston Green, Birmingham.

Mike Johnson and **Sylvia Phillips**, Manchester Metropolitan University.

Tessa Knott, Primary Class Teacher.

Lindsay Peer, British Dyslexia Association.

Rita Silvester, Adviser for Special Education Needs, Education Service, Derby City Council.

Chris D. Smith and **Helen E. Whiteley**, Department of Psychology, University of Central Lancashire.

Dorothy Smith, Advisory Teacher for Specific Learning Difficulties, Suffolk, and Chair of Publications Sub-Committee, NASEN.

Pauline M. Smith, Primary Class Teacher.

Special Needs Teaching Service, Leicestershire.

Janet Spencer and **Joan Collins**, Sandwell CENT team, Sandwell, West Midlands.

Susy Stone, Bell Lane Primary, Hendon, London.

Jane Vaughan, Freemantles School, Chertsey, Surrey.

Patricia Wilde, John Bentley School, Calne, Wiltshire.

Sue Webb and **Louise Wood**, Tewkesbury School, Tewkesbury, Gloucestershire.

The New Genre Nation

It's nine-o-five and on the mat
Laura's loving Literacy Hour,
her body straight,
pulled forward by its power.
Clipped to the board are untold tales
and poetry as well,
Miss Corbett points her magic wand
and Laura's in her spell.

Graham's grappling with graphemes,
his sight words almost done;
Beth is bored, (Better at number,
my dear? Your hour will come).
Robert dreams he's a giant Theosaurus -
he's rotund, rubicund, rosy and red!
Joe has never ever listened -
he's designing hoovers in his head.
Cory's cursing Snot! Blot! Grot!,
stabbing his neighbour, wasting no time,
he's practising onset and crime.

It's nine-three-five and at his table,
pale as a worksheet, blank as a page,
Brian is independently unable.
He's forgotten his task
his bladder is bursting,
but he's sat by the sign that says 'Don't ask.'

Imogen's imagining imagery,
Gladys is empathising, gladly;
J.T.'s abbreviating acronymically,
and E.T's phoneme home.
Chantelle's chanting nursery rhymes
and Simon's rhymin' madly.
Cate finds korrespondence konfusing,
S-a-m was blended at birth,
and Lisa's
          listing
            badly.
Dexter's text-level headed and
William knows what a Wordsworth.

It's nine-five-five and at the back
Tommy's troubled by teacher talk.
It fills his ears,
it fills his head,
his legs are numb,
his brain is dead,
his eyes are dull from all that sharing,
his body retreating, back and back,
his hands are bored, his fingers tearing
at his velcro shoes. A fruitless hour
and, with his luck, a fruitless playtime too.

Miss Corbett panics with Pre-SATs-Tension,
she peels off a post-it and clozes her i's,
and wonders will they ever parse?
(Lord, beam me up to another dimension.
Could even Big Reggie teach this class?)

Only Brian welcomes the plenary time -
                he's onamata peeing.

© *Kate Farminer*

PART ONE: SPECIAL SCHOOLS
Special School Responses: 'Flexibility and Individuality'

Dorothy Smith

Fourteen special schools contributed to this section whereas others sent in fuller responses. Five of the former were from schools for Severe Learning Difficulties (SLD) and Profound and Multiple Learning Difficulties (PMLD) who catered for an age-range of 3-16 years. One contribution was from a Conductive Education Centre, another from a school for autistic children of primary age, another from a speech and language unit giving part-time provision for 14 children and another from a school for children with physical and neurological impairment. The others ranged from an infants' special school to returns from class teachers in various types of special schools.

Pupils' special educational needs and their particular problems in coping with the Hour

As would be expected a diverse range of special educational needs were outlined and most schools mentioned that there were added behavioural problems alongside communication problems, sensory impairments, severe learning difficulties, developmental delay and physical impairment. Because of the range of learning and special needs the responses outlined the schools' particular problems posed by their children coping with the Literacy Hour. For example, one response felt that literacy work for those pupils with PMLD who function at around a 3-6 month level was hardly appropriate because of their almost non-existent communication. A school for SLD pupils found that because small groups had diverse problems it was difficult to work with them within the whole class organisation. The speech and language unit noted that because the pupils' understanding of the language of grammar is poor, terminology must be explained beforehand and continually reinforced. The curriculum manager at the school for children with physical and neurological impairment explained that her own class of eight pupils ranging from Years 4 to 7 contains three who use communication aids in the form of Cameleons plus Mayers Johnson symbols and the fourth uses symbols plus a Big Mack Switch plus Yes/No answers. These pupils are physically unable to handle books or speak because of their cerebral palsy. She is using the communication aids to help these pupils access stories etc.

Poor concentration and attention, limited understanding, working independently and difficulties in ensuring progression because of older children working from the Reception Level were other problem areas but even the infants' school felt that by starting with short snappy sessions at the beginning of the year the children were able to sustain the full Hour by the following July. This was also noted by another school where their youngest children managed 15 minutes whilst those in Years 4, 5 and 6 built up to coping with the whole Hour. One school found the time constraints of the Hour meant that children did not always finish their set work and then became upset when another activity was suggested. (This problem is later echoed in the responses from mainstream schools.)

A particular problem noted by the Conductive Education Centre was in creating the right balance in the whole class shared text work. They had to find something appropriate for a child working at nursery level alongside others who were older. Although many of their children progressed quicker with reading and even with spelling their particular problems with the physical skill of handwriting meant that they had to use alternative means of recording such as the use of computers. Therefore, learning is slower for these children than their counterparts in the mainstream.

Literacy Hour arrangements

The varied descriptions of these schools' arrangements because of their particular circumstances make it difficult to show any consensus. However, most use the whole class shared text routine which seems to work well. One school felt that a five-minute plenary was the optimum length of time. 'Story retell' was the main focus of a primary special school and this made use of the same book repeatedly with groups focusing on similar but differentiated tasks. One PMLD/SLD school worked on a rolling programme based on Big Books but noted that pupils with more complex needs will work within the Hour as appropriate. However, there is emphasis for these children on sensory and early communication skills. Another school for SLD explained that initially the Hour was a departmental session to allow for differentiation and was mainly focused on story, drama and poetry but now it includes reading and writing.

There have been adaptations such as some pupils working in groups for about 15 minutes or so whilst others need a 1:1 situation in which to function. Another school found that some classes could cope with an hour as a block whereas other classes had to spread the Literacy Hour over the day in 15 or 20-minute units. Groups are small and often based on ability level. One school mentioned that it was 'working towards' the Literacy Hour especially if the main aim for some pupils is functional communication of basic needs.

Strategies to overcome problems

These schools have obviously worked hard to see how they can make the Literacy Hour work to their advantage. They note the problems and seek to overcome these. These schools haven't rushed into the Hour lightly and as one school wrote, its staff had spent a great deal of time and effort in making the *National Literacy Strategy* appropriate through an audit of good practice within the school. Similarly, before starting to implement the strategy the school for Conductive Education decided to adapt it to making the writing side relevant to children with physical disabilities. For example, it added in methods by which the children could learn to write (such as Clicker Plus). Staff altered texts for whole class shared text work to suit the differences in children and extra sensory input was added (such as the use of symbols). The use of visual prompts, multi-sensory approaches and the use of objects of reference (such as photos, pictures and lots of practical tasks) were found to be necessary and were mentioned in most responses. Books and accompanying games and activities had to be very visual and interesting. The teacher-in-charge of the speech and language unit found that the pupils were capable of completing literacy strategy tasks as long as they were provided with time, visual prompts, drama (eg opportunities to act out stories etc.) and many reinforcement activities (especially questioning). These children found it harder to cope within their mainstream classes.

High staff ratio is given in the special schools. This is needed to keep children on task and to make sure that groups do not work unsupervised. This use of additional adults was frequently mentioned and the additional work from Special Support Assistants and Nursery Nurses was applauded. One SLD school explained that the introduction of reading and writing in an accessible way for their school population had made target setting easier for teachers. Their Learning Support Assistants are being trained by the Literacy Co-ordinator to deliver reading and writing activities as the eventual aim is that all staff members will be so trained and then regardless of absences or movement of staff throughout the school the pupils' progress will not be affected.

Resource implications

From the suggestions given in this section it could be seen how hard these teachers in special schools work in order to make the Literacy Hour work, as well as how necessary it is felt to spend as much money as is possible.

- Purchasing non-fiction texts with good quality pictures with minimal text can be a great expense but well worth it.
- Buying lots of Big Books is worth the expense.

- Writing of own books is helpful because of the difficulties in catering for a wide range of abilities. (Most schools noted that staff produced their own materials and wrote books which were suitable for their pupils.)
- Lamination of 'home-made' materials makes them last longer.
- Using overhead projectors, Velcro boards, white boards and magnetic boards.
- Buying as many resources such as visual aids, games, rhymes, tapes etc. is necessary.
- Searching for appropriate texts with lower reading ages is needed.
- The Conductive Education Centre found modelling writing on the computer successful for whole class shared text writing as it was one of the children's main accesses to writing. But this would only work with a very small class as all children need to be able to see the computer. It would be good if there could be some way to project the screen image or to use a larger TV to display the image.
- Big Books which contain stories for acting out are valuable.
- Less money spent on books and more on high-tech equipment can give pupils the opportunity to 'speak' and turn-take.
- If pupils find it hard to focus on the Big Books then more copies of smaller books are useful.

Concluding remarks

These were very positive and can be linked to the articles elsewhere in this book where other writers also show how the Literacy Hour can have a positive effect in specialised settings.

- The primary area special school Special Educational Needs Co-ordinator (SENCO) felt that it was very hard work to read all the materials and adapt these for use in school and also to maintain positive 'vibes' for the other staff members. However, because of the enjoyment derived by the staff and pupils she has felt that the Literacy Hour is working.
- The school for autistic children has seen improvement in literacy skills, in particular one child's improvement in his/her ability to control use of language. The school is starting a group to work on the Additional Literacy Support (ALS) Module 1 and will assess before and after a term to see if there is any measured improvement.
- The infants' special school felt that it could have been very easy to say that the Hour couldn't be achieved. With careful planning and thought staff have shown the way in which the children have developed through the ever-progressing Hour. Although at a slower rate from the mainstream, the children's reading and writing skills have developed.
- The Conductive Education Centre has found the *National Literacy Strategy* invaluable as an aid to teaching. However, as always children with special educational needs such as physical disabilities have not been considered in the initial national work, and learning rates for these children differ even within different areas of literacy development.
- One of the schools for SLD pupils has found that the Literacy Hour has worked well and this was noted in a recent inspection report as a strength.
- A special school with an original MLD designation wrote that the *National Literacy Strategy* has provided a very good and useful structure. Although there were initial misgivings about the level of planning and preparation work required, there has been a positive response from pupils and teachers. The former enjoy the Big Books and the text interaction. The latter feel that there have been some problems fitting in time for writing work and some teachers have been unsure about communication and how to plan for speaking and listening.
- A school for PMLD/SLD reported many initial positive indicators. Staff believe the children are enjoying it and the Literacy Hour is also aiding the presentation of English throughout the school, thus improving consistency.

- Another of the schools for SLD pupils related 'There are very few children within this school who are not working on pre-reading activities and to our surprise and delight we have some non-verbal children reading and others working towards it.'
- The school for children with physical and neurological impairment has previously organised a similar system to the Hour in the school and has found that the Literacy Hour has focused planning and resources. Even though there are many children with physical disabilities within the primary department the staff are finding ways of delivering the Literacy Hour effectively.

A Multi-Modal Approach to Literacy

Professor Barry Carpenter

Introduction

The advent of the Literacy Hour has triggered much debate amongst teachers with responsibility for children with severe learning difficulties (SLD). Few would argue with the rationale for the Literacy Hour, which is 'designed to provide a practical structure of time and class management' (DfEE, 1998a). Alongside the rationale, however, must come the issue of relevance.

An initial response to the word 'literacy' in the context of the curriculum would, for most teachers, assume a comfortable feel. Indeed, prior to the implementation of the English National Curriculum, it was the curriculum heading most commonly used to describe this area of learning in SLD education. The structure of the Literacy Hour, based on short intensive bursts of various literacy-based activities, is well matched to the learning needs of many children with severe learning difficulties. The guidance offered in the 'management of literacy at school level' (DfEE, 1998b) recommends that the teaching strategies to support literacy instruction are: directing, demonstrating, explaining, guiding investigations, listening and observing, evaluation and assessing etc., all of which would be features of effective teaching for children with severe learning difficulties.

Interpreting the Literacy Hour

To do this, we need to marshal all that we know about how children with severe learning difficulties acquire literacy skills. The literature agrees on the need to provide consistent models of literacy use for these children. Many writers assert that print (in all of its forms) must have a high profile in the learner's environment and must be granted high status through frequent use in a variety of purposeful activities (Koppenhaver & Yoder, 1991). Often it has been found that literacy has a low priority within the curriculum and situations existed where writing tools were rarely accessible to children. We have learnt much in the last two decades about the acquisition of literacy skills through a variety of alternative approaches (Bishop, Rankin & Mirenda, 1994). Indeed there are now conclusive studies which would demonstrate that some children with severe learning difficulties will not acquire language and literacy skills through conventional means; their brain functioning may require alternative methods (Buckley, 1985).

Visual languages (signs and symbols)

Visual clueing methods (eg objects of reference, photographs, pictures etc.) have contributed much to the development of literacy skills in children with SLD. Sue Buckley (1985) has written extensively on the use of whole-word approaches in reading to stimulate language in children with Down's syndrome. Other studies have clearly indicated how signing can not only form a viable communication mode for children with severe learning difficulties, but how it can provide a route to literacy also (Carpenter, 1991). Symbols have made a considerable contribution to literacy and the wider curriculum (Detheridge & Detheridge, 1997; Carpenter, Ashdown & Bovair, 1996). Objects of reference offer an excellent means of establishing not only a communication system for children at a very early developmental level, but also of securely rooting the conceptual foundation of each linguistic concept (Park, 1998).

'English lessons'

In planning for the implementation of the Literacy Hour, we need to be mindful of the lessons learnt from implementing English in the National Curriculum (Hinchcliffe, 1996). Again, a process of curriculum adaptation and modification is essential if we are to ensure that the curriculum is suitably enriched and meaningful for the child with SLD. There has been some consternation that the guidance issued on the Literacy Hour to date has not addressed the needs of this pupil group. Teachers are often heard arguing about the complexity and diversity of children with severe learning difficulties, but, providing we are given a climate where it is appropriate to extend the national guidelines without fear of chastisement, then school-based development is probably the best way to ensure that the needs of our highly diverse individuals are met. A rigid interpretation of the Literacy Hour would not be helpful; we need to redefine the Literacy Hour in the light of the learning needs of our children and what we know about effective teaching. Hence, it is realistic to assume that many of the language, communication and cognition goals for our children can be achieved through the vehicle of literacy.

Finding a framework

This is the stance we have adopted at Sunfield School. Any skilled teacher of children with severe learning difficulties knows that their classroom is a diverse learning environment supporting a range of needs in their pupils. Therefore we asked ourselves what, within the context of literacy, do we want our children, who have severe and complex needs, to learn? Is the Literacy Hour an appropriate vehicle that can aid teaching and learning styles rather than convoluting the classroom experience?

We sought answers to these questions by thinking of *one* common concept that we could present to our children. Taking the concept (eg 'house'), we looked at the variety of the ways that this concept could be presented in all its forms to the children through differentiated teaching. Not only were we seeking ways of input to the children, but all of the ways that they could indicate emerging knowledge and understanding of the concept (output). Below, *Figure 1* illustrates the outcomes of this discussion.

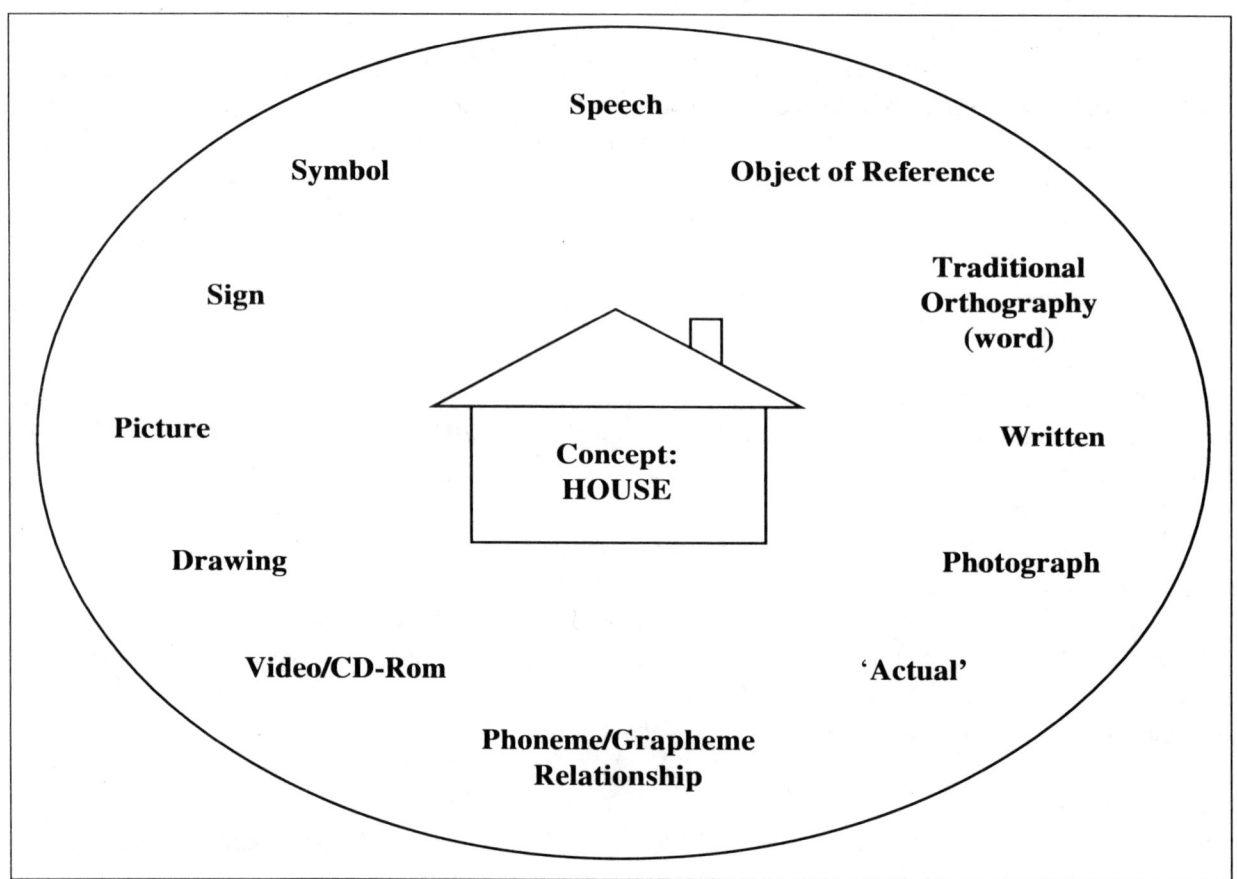

Figure 1: An Example of a Multi-Tiered Approach to Literacy - Outcome of Staff Training Workshop, Sunfield School (April 1998).

What emerged was that literacy in the SLD setting necessitates a multi-tiered approach - there can be no one way of presenting a concept to the children. A variety of strategies using sign, symbol, objects of reference, sensory channels must run alongside the presentation in all of its spoken, graphic and real dimensions. This definition will range from presenting the concept in its object form to its written form, from its signed form to its spoken form. It will embrace learning for the child in the areas of picture recognition, object matching, word building and spelling to name but a few. Teaching will be through a variety of media - pictorial, video, CD-ROM and computer-assisted. A rigorous analysis of the presentation opportunities of each concept will enable *every* child to access that concept at a level appropriate to them. Further, it will indicate progression within the concept in a linear as well as hierarchical form. This will ensure that each child receives a relevant, needs-based approach and remains an active participant within the literacy learning experience. With all of these teaching and learning variants, classroom management becomes a key issue. A framework, which offers guidance, structure and focus for teacher and learner becomes crucial.

The literacy clock (DfEE, 1998a) is a visually helpful framework; the short bursts of teaching are wholly appropriate, but require modification if the Literacy Hour for children with SLD is to remain relevant. The content of each session (eg reading, writing or word work) needs a broader definition than that provided in the Literacy Hour guidance. Embodied within a model relevant to the child with SLD needs to be a clear acknowledgement that many of our children communicate through augmentative approaches. These approaches are the learning and communication modes through which our children operate daily in each of their environments. Indeed they may have a multiplicity of modes.

Taking the structure of the Literacy Hour, we 'retimed' the clock to a pattern more appropriate to the child with SLD. To ensure that our model remained child-centred, the model was set within a plan-do-review cycle. Whole class, small group, individual teaching and independent learning are still embodied within our model. This approach gave us the opportunity to identify skills fundamental to the learning growth of children with SLD. Skills such as visual discrimination, visual closure, auditory memory and auditory recall were set within the context of a curriculum initiative which was presented for all children. As ever, the challenge to the teacher was access to that curriculum domain (Carpenter et al., 1996). These essential skill areas afforded the children learning routes into literacy that ensured relevance.

Implementing the model

Once the model was established, there was a need to identify the activities that would support its implementation. The Curriculum Manager, in conjunction with the Literacy Co-ordinators, prepared guidance sheets which took the model section by section and suggested a range of activities that would be appropriate to the individual children in each class group. These activities were linked with the school Programme of Study for English. An example of an activity for each section of the multi-modal Literacy Hour is given in Table 1.

To facilitate many activities within the Literacy Hour, further resource identification was necessary. For example, the tactile stories beautifully produced by Chris Fuller (1990) have become invaluable for Big Book work for those children with more profound and multiple learning difficulties. Writing with symbols, either through computer-aided (available from Widget Software) or indeed free hand, have developed not only creative writing skills in children, but also fine motor skills (Carpenter & Detheridge, 1993). As ever, there was a need to make materials. The acquisition of traditional orthography is a well-documented challenge for students with severe learning difficulties. Symbols can offer a 'perceptual bridge' (Carpenter, 1991) which can aid the transition for the student from picture through symbol to word.

The activities were tested through lesson planning for each section of the Literacy Hour. These lesson plans stated learning intentions, teaching activity, resources, learning outcomes and class organisation. Links were made to the Individual Education Care Plans for each child, which always contain termly literacy priority targets. Records were kept to assess student learning over time. These lesson plans will enable a full evaluation of the effectiveness of the Literacy Hour to take place later in the academic year.

SECTION	ACTIVITY	LEARNING GOAL	MATERIAL DEVELOPMENT
Whole class	Big Book sharing	To identify key words/symbols in a story	Books from our Library Resources have been colour photocopied and enlarged. Symbols have been inserted to supplement the text. Each page has been mounted on to A4 card and laminated. Tactile stories, commercially produced by Chris Fuller (1993), have also been used.
Small groups/ individuals (Writing)	Creative writing	To compose a short story	During National Children's Book Week (1998), children were introduced to a storyteller. They were then encouraged to 'tell' someone their story. This was either recorded for them or the student wrote their story in symbols using Widgit Software's 'Writing with Symbols' programme. These books were bound, catalogued and placed in the school library.
Small groups/ individuals (Word Work)	Word/symbol recognition/ naming	To identify key words	A dictionary box was developed as a class resource. Students who had grasped the initial letter of a word could locate this in the box. To 'cue' them into the whole word, each word card contained a symbol clue and the graphic version.
Small groups/ individuals (Reading)	Sentence construction	To construct a sentence in its spoken, symbolled, signed or written forms	Children selected words/symbols from a word bank hung on the wall to use on a large wooden sentence-maker. They would compose a sentence which was then spoken and/or signed and then represented in a graphic form (symbol/word).
Whole group (Recall Session)	Sign/symbol word of the week	To acquire a new language concept in its oral, visual or graphic form	To reflect the range of ability within any class group, it was possible to differentiate the teaching of a single language concept by presenting it as an object (tactile form), photograph, symbol, sign or written word.

Table 1: Activity Examples.

The concluding part of any lesson always focuses on the achievements of individual children, when they could review the cycle of literacy learning they had engaged in during the previous hour. Many students enjoyed having a new language concept each week to acquire in any of its forms - through object or picture recognition, in its signed form, or through symbol/word recognition. This simple focus meant that many students could measure their own progress in the course of the five days, which was a great source of stimulus.

Conclusion

As for all teachers in the country, this is very much a development year for the *National Literacy Strategy*. The Literacy Hour as the major vehicle for the delivery of the Strategy needs ongoing evaluation. This article reports the first phase of development at Sunfield School. To date, our initial conclusions would be that the Literacy Hour, if constructed sensitively to the needs of children with severe learning difficulties, has a high degree of relevance. The style of delivery is well matched to the learning pattern of our children. Children's learning needs are directly informing curriculum resource development. There is much making of books and resource preparation, and it certainly would be helpful if books in an appropriate format and with symbol support could be commercially produced.

The focus on literacy has encouraged teachers to participate in events such as National Children's Book Week, and to make this a relevant experience for children of all abilities in our school through a range of artefacts, sensory materials, assistive technologies, as well as books in various media. In-service training is ongoing with focused sessions to date on Big Books, shared reading and augmentative communication, in addition to using the training resources provided as part of the *National Literacy Strategy*.

The right style of Literacy Hour enables true learning goals to be met and their teachers to achieve the successful teaching indicators - 'interactive, well-paced, confident and ambitious Literacy Hours' (DfEE, 1998a) - outlined in the *National Literacy Strategy*. For this to have relevance for children with severe learning difficulties, we have to acknowledge that literacy has to be multi-modal, and that its delivery comes through a variety of augmented strategies. At Sunfield, this multi-modal approach has led us to evolve Augmented Literacy as the means by which all our pupils engage in the *National Literacy Strategy*. If we can achieve this, then we have something truly meaningful to offer our children. For as Michael Williams (1995), an augmentative communication user, reminds us:

I awake, surrounded by the familiar things of life,
Saved by high octane literacy.
I am here with you,
Empowered by the written word.

Acknowledgement

The author would like to acknowledge the ideas shared by Sunfield teaching staff in the development of this article.

References

Bishop, K., Rankin, J. and Mirenda, P. (1994) 'Impact of graphic symbol use on reading acquisition', *Augmentative and Alternative Communication*, 10, 113-125.
Buckley, S. (1985) 'Attaining basic education skills: reading, writing and number', in D. Lane and B. Stratford (Eds) *Current Approaches to Down's Syndrome*. East Sussex: Holt, Reinehart & Winston.
Carpenter, B. (1991) 'Unlocking the door: Access to English in the National Curriculum for children with severe learning difficulties', in B. Smith (Ed.) *Interactive Approaches to Teaching the Core Subjects*. Birmingham: Lame Duck Publishing.
Carpenter, B. and Detheridge, T. (1993) 'Writing with Symbols', *Support for Learning* 9, 1, 27-32.
Carpenter, B., Ashdown, R. and Bovair, K. (Eds) (1996) *Enabling Access: Effective teaching and learning for pupils with learning difficulties*. London: David Fulton.
Department for Education and Employment (1998a) *The National Literacy Strategy: Framework for teaching*. London: DfEE.
Department for Education and Employment (1998b) *The National Literacy Strategy: The management of literacy at School Level*. London: DfEE.
Detheridge, T. and Detheridge, M. (1997) *Literacy through Symbols*. London: David Fulton.
Fuller, C. (1990) *Tactile Stories*. London: Resources of Learning Difficulties: The Consortium.
Hinchcliffe, V. (1996) 'English', in B. Carpenter, R. Ashdown and K. Bovair (Eds) *Enabling Access: Effective teaching and learning for pupils with learning difficulties*. London: David Fulton.
Koppenhaver, D. A. and Yoder, D. E. (1991) 'Literacy issues in persons with severe speech and physical impairments', in R. Gaylord-Ross (Ed.) *Issues and Research in Special Education (Vol. 2)*. New York: Columbia University, Teachers College Press.
Park, K. (1998) 'Form and function in Early Communication', *The SLD Experience* 21, 2-5.
Williams, M. (1995) 'Outcomes of AAC', *Augmentative Communication News* 8.5.
Widgit Software, 102 Radford Road, Leamington Spa CV31 1LF (Tel. 01926 885303).

Freemantles School: Structure of the Literacy Hour for Children with Autistic Spectrum Disorders in Specialised Provision

Jane Vaughan

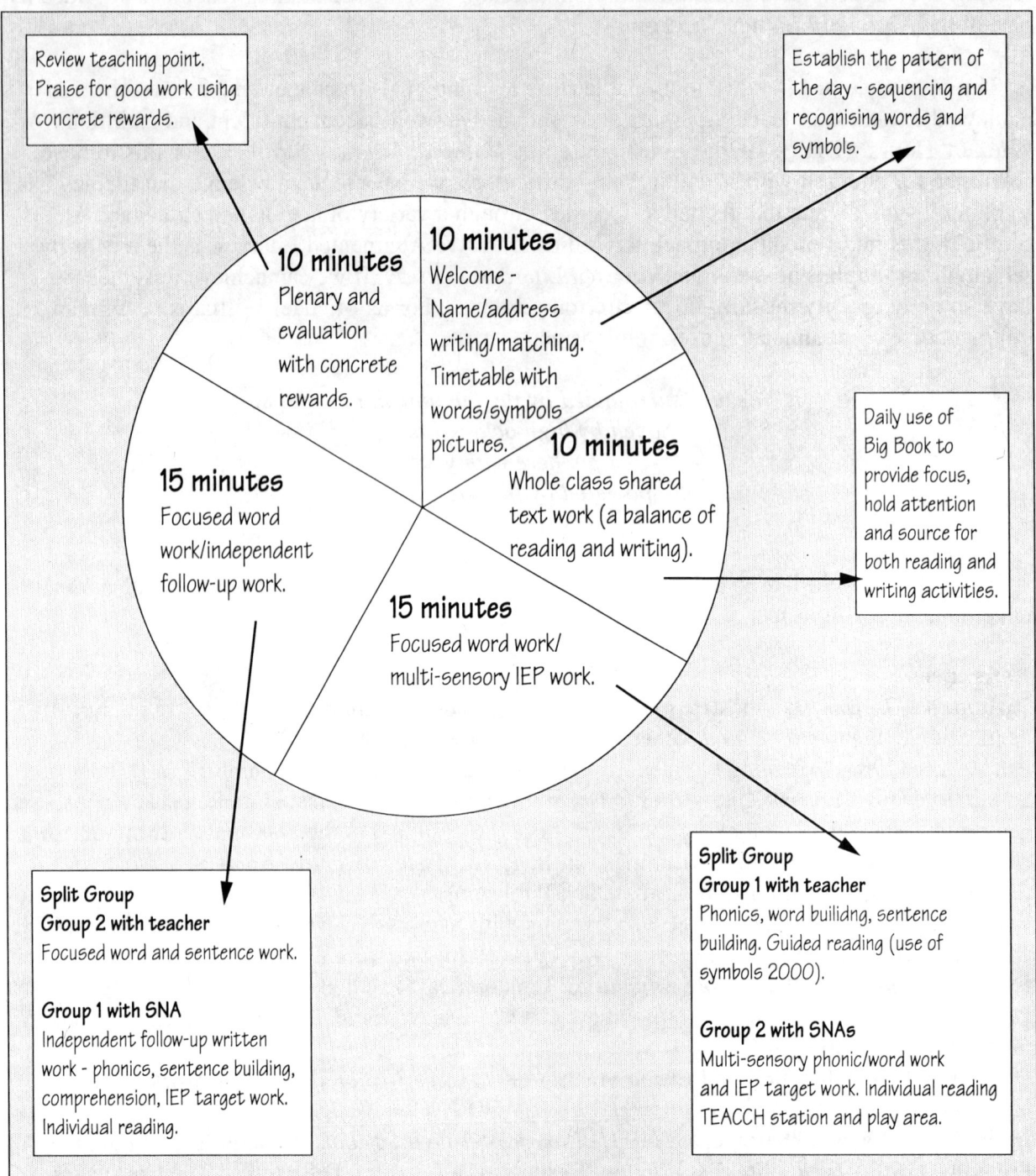

Review teaching point. Praise for good work using concrete rewards.

Establish the pattern of the day - sequencing and recognising words and symbols.

10 minutes Plenary and evaluation with concrete rewards.

10 minutes Welcome - Name/address writing/matching. Timetable with words/symbols pictures.

10 minutes Whole class shared text work (a balance of reading and writing).

15 minutes Focused word work/independent follow-up work.

15 minutes Focused word work/ multi-sensory IEP work.

Daily use of Big Book to provide focus, hold attention and source for both reading and writing activities.

Split Group
Group 2 with teacher
Focused word and sentence work.

Group 1 with SNA
Independent follow-up written work - phonics, sentence building, comprehension, IEP target work. Individual reading.

Split Group
Group 1 with teacher
Phonics, word builidng, sentence building. Guided reading (use of symbols 2000).

Group 2 with SNAs
Multi-sensory phonic/word work and IEP target work. Individual reading TEACCH station and play area.

The model

The model of the Literacy Hour which has been used assumes a group in which a range of abilities and concentration spans will be contained. For this reason a split group is used, in order to accommodate the differences and show the use of support staff complementing the work of the teacher. For some groups it may not be possible to carry out these activities concurrently - the Hour may need to be divided so that activities take place at different points within the school day, punctuated by physical activity.

Welcome

All students with an ASD (Autistic Spectrum Disorder) will need to know the plan of the day. This time should be used to establish the group; it will be necessary to think about where in the group each child is seated and where the SNA (Special Needs Assistant) help is positioned; also necessary will be clear, simple language delivered in short sentences. The activity may include name matching (Velcro-backed labels), name writing on a whiteboard, or writing name and address on a template. The plan of the day should be established by the use of a visual timetable, whether in words, symbols or photographs. This should be used as a group reading opportunity.

Whole class shared text work (reading and writing)

Reading

Shared text will be from a Big Book. Students should be reminded each time of the rules of group work (with symbols if necessary) - good sitting, good looking, good listening. It will be necessary to constantly refocus each child on to the book by using individual names and non-verbal prompts from SNAs (SNAs should be careful not to be drawn into an interaction with a student, but to use signing, or single words if really necessary, to direct the student back to the teacher). As the text is read, attention will be drawn to the teaching point for the day. This may be through highlighting text, covering text or matching text with word or phonic cards. Careful thought should be given to differentiation so that all students are involved and participate.

Writing

It is in this area that the ASD child will have most difficulty. The deficit includes not only an impairment of expressive language, but also an impairment of imagination. Students will need to become familiar with the text before it can be used to develop writing. The development may take this form:

- naming an object or a person;
- creating a two-word phrase;
- creating a three-word phrase;
- creating simple sentences.

These will all be related to the visual stimuli within the shared text. Sentences should be built co-operatively within the group setting, starting with word cards, progressing to sentences written on the whiteboard and, where able, on to sentences written in books or on paper. When these skills are established, pictures and words can be used to develop prediction, which can then be developed to project an idea; the regular practice of this skill, with good oral and visual prompts from the teacher, will lead to the development of imagination. Appropriate words, as tools, should always be on hand in some form, whether in a list, on a board or on cards, perhaps with symbols. Teacher input should be sensitive, allowing a student sufficient time to formulate thoughts, but always providing a prompt to prevent a student from floundering and feeling inadequate - success must be built in to this activity.

Teacher-led sessions - style
- Use of multi-sensory resources (taking care not to over-stimulate);
- Use of clear visual aids - letter cards, word cards, symbols. Make sure they are large enough for all the students in the group to see clearly;
- Small group - half the original class; close proximity to teacher and boards in order to be able to handle materials easily for word building, sentence building etc.;
- Keep language minimal and simple;
- Model activities before asking students to carry them out.

Follow-up work

This will be an extension of the lesson content at the appropriate level, either with SNA support or at an independent level.

Multi-sensory work

Students with SLD will require this approach to extension work; activities should include cutting and sticking; letter and word making using dough, foam, rice, lentils, cornflour paste, jelly; listening to and singing songs, watching appropriate video material; using a play environment such as the playground or soft play to find and match letters and words.

Independent work

- Independent work may be more successful if a workstation is provided.
- Think about positioning. Sides may cut out distractions, as may having a child's back to the rest of the class.
- Provide the student with visual prompt - eg a sign saying **I am working on my own**, but also provide **Help please** option on the back of the sign.
- Model expected outcome for students so that they really know what to do.
- Break down tasks into small steps. Make sure it is clear when the task is finished. It may be helpful to have a 'finished' box in which to put finished work.
- Visually define the time a task is expected to take using a clock or a timer.
- Use SNA/adult helper to give regular prompts to stay on task.
- Make sure the student knows the 'rules' for working independently.

Plenary session

- This session should be as positive as possible.
- Students should be reminded again of the teaching point of the day.
- Praise should be given for following 'rules' of behaviour, as well as work.
- Visual/concrete rewards should be given as well as verbal praise for success.

The Literacy Hour at Merstone School

Elaine Holland

Merstone is a school for children with severe learning difficulties aged between 2 and 19 years. There are at the time of writing 67 students on role, working within seven integrated classes, including a Nursery and Assessment Unit and a post-16 group. Merstone encompasses the National Curriculum subjects supplemented by a specific curriculum designed for pupils with severe learning difficulties. The Literacy Co-ordinator for the school is also the class teacher for the Reception/Key Stage 1 class which presently consists of eight children between the ages of 4 and 7 years, all of whom present widely varying severe and challenging learning difficulties.

The Literacy Hour arrangements

Throughout the school, children remain with their class group for literacy work, which is predominantly organised by the class teacher who differentiates activities as appropriate. The class teacher also organises Special Support Assistants to work with small groups and support the class session ensuring effective and stimulating teaching and learning situations.

In general the overall format of the Literacy Hour is followed for the majority of the specific literacy situations (ie a whole class introduction, small group workshops and a plenary). The sessions are planned to ensure that the needs of all the children are met and small group work is often highly differentiated to encompass the great variety of cognitive, physical and emotional needs of the pupils.

Teaching is dynamic and innovative, using a great variety or resources (commercial, hand-made and improvised), and assessment and recording varies according to the activity and the pupil concerned. Recently the school has developed the role of the curriculum support teacher to encompass literacy, and she supports individuals and small groups with very specific targets.

SEN pupils

The school population presents a wide range of severe learning difficulties, including pupils with profound and multiple difficulties, those with severely challenging behaviour, pupils on the autistic spectrum, pupils with multi-sensory impairments and those with speech and language difficulties. Staff work extremely hard to meet the needs of all these pupils and deliver a broad and balanced curriculum which is made accessible to all. The same is true with the Literacy Hour and staff are constantly exploring new and effective ways to deliver literacy to SEN pupils. This obviously has implications for resources; including time and staff management, physical resources (effective and ineffective commercial tools), etc.

Generally stimulating, large equipment works well, especially if it is clear and simple. Sensory equipment is often helpful (ie if it has an auditory or tactile element), as this can be used for pupils with multi-sensory impairments or to hold the attention of pupils with short concentration spans.

Commercially good equipment is hard to come by, and often it is the case that staff 'make' resources relevant to the literacy focus and appropriate for the needs of individual pupils. As a school team, staff share these resources and ideas and support colleagues with resourcing needs. At present the school is building up a bank of multi-sensory resource kits to accompany books used within the Literacy Hour (often Big Books), and these are kept as a central resource for all to use.

Other pointers

On the whole, the Literacy Hour is working well within the school and staff are keen and enthusiastic, working hard to ensure they meet their pupils' individual needs. However, as special schools have pointed out, it must be made clear that time and acknowledgement should be given to the needs of SEN pupils in all Government legislation. This is particularly so for those with severe learning difficulties working within special school environments where resources are required to be specialised, where teaching and learning styles are altered, and where individual expectations may be very different. This is the case with the *National Literacy Strategy* where it has been due to the dedication, expertise and willingness of individual teachers that it has been a success.

The Literacy Hour at Aspen Unit, Whitfield School

Nick Andrews and Anita Lundy-Overton

Aspen Unit is a unit for children with severe and profound multiple learning difficulties attached to a primary school. There are 40 children aged 3 to 11 years.

The Literacy Profile has been developed from work by the SLD schools (Kent) Literacy Consortium (see Appendix 1). Permission has been given to reproduce this.

Literacy approaches in primary schools have resulted in an anti-inclusion or certainly in restricted opportunities for our children, hence our need to develop our own policy. The policy has resulted from the failure of all departments (local and national) to give advice on how to proceed.

Literacy Strategy Policy
1. Statement of intent
In adopting the *National Literacy Strategy* it is the intention to raise standards of literacy in the Aspen Unit.

Literacy skills in the unit are defined as the capacity to communicate through signing, speaking, listening, reading and writing (for a range of purposes).

While committed to raising standards generally, the unit staff reserve the right to differentiate the programme to accommodate the pupils' very specific needs, so that pupils are set realistic and appropriate targets. The pupils' education and well-being is the principal concern.

2. Approach towards the Literacy Strategy
'Communication and Literacy' starts with eye pointing, body language (relaxation), facial expression and Makaton signing. It then progresses through speaking and listening skills to reading and writing in both symbol and written word format.

Methods and aids include the use of real objects (objects of reference), photographs, Makaton signs and symbols, songs, tapes, music, computer games and programmes, sensory aids, books and traditional writing equipment.

Means of delivering literacy will include whole class teaching for short periods, small group teaching and individual teaching where necessary, in line with the National Strategy guidance. Any subject or topic is covered using a variety of approaches to promote maximum involvement of children with frequent changes of pace and classroom setting. Subjects are covered in short periods but are constantly revised and revisited to help refresh and stimulate learning.

3. Approach to the Literacy 'Hour'
The short concentration span of most children within the unit deems the length of the Literacy 'Hour' as often being too long. Therefore, the 'Hour' is constructed to tie in with the needs of pupils and varies in time. Teaching of literacy is broken down into short manageable time spans.

At Key Stage 1: The children are at the early stages of literacy development and therefore the content is appropriate to their developmental level and age.

- Whole class teaching for approximately 20 minutes each day. Areas included: symbol timetable, days of the week, responding to register, initial letter sounds.
- Stories (including sensory stories) in small groups or one to one.

- Daily small group or one-to-one work: Pre-reading - matching, sorting etc. Pre-writing - marks on paper, pencil control, writing patterns, tracing etc., emergent writing.

At Key Stage 2: It is envisaged that the Literacy Strategy will be delivered as a block period at least three times a week and in addition carried through on a cross-curricular basis. These block sessions are complemented with short, literacy-specific, and individual or small group sessions.

Current Key Stage 2 blocks are:

- Session 1: Speaking and Listening, News and Writing etc.
- Session 2: Stories and Books.
- Session 3: Phonics.

4. Content of programme

Speaking - Verbal expression

Children are encouraged to take part in one-to-one conversations, to relate news to a group, ie circle time, 'big group', to speak to the whole school in assembly, drama etc., to use the telephone and to convey spoken messages. Singing is also used intensively to encourage verbal expression at the earliest stage. Speech therapy is provided through identified needs. Makaton signing and symbols are used to support and encourage speech and language. Makaton provides a means of expression for certain children whose verbal expression is underdeveloped.

Listening - Taking in messages aurally

Activities such as conversation, verbal instruction, music, tapes, story telling, theatre visits, drama and assembly are available to all children. In addition Music Therapy and Speech and Language Therapy will be available to those requiring alternative additional input.

Reading - deciphering visual messages

In this area materials will cover songs, rhymes, poetry, greeting cards and letters, instructions, warning and information. This is in addition to traditional reading schemes (*Oxford Reading Tree*, *Ginn 360*, both in symbol and word form). Makaton symbols and photographs are used to enhance messages.

Handwriting - Leaving permanent messages or marks

In the first instance children are encouraged to make marks with a variety of materials. Handwriting skills are developed through fingerprints, computer printout, Makaton symbols or traditional written word (tracing, copying, independent writing).

Creative writing - Communication of thoughts and ideas in a permanent form

Creative writing is established using pictures, symbols, emergent writing, computer printouts, pencil and paper. This may involve the use of a scribe.

5. Mechanics of teaching

- Progressing from Makaton signing and symbol reading to traditional reading and writing are taught via word building and recognition, sentence structure and early grammatical concepts.
- Word recognition - through use of flash cards, wordbooks and constant and frequent exposure to common words, eg days of the week, children's names etc.
- Word building (spelling) - taught through attention to phonics, word patterns and rhymes, letter recognition and formation - both lower and upper case.
- Sentence structure - the importance of capital letters at the beginning and full stop at the end. In the early stages of development, the 'start and finish' concept is through signs and symbols.
- Grammar - concentration on nouns, verbs, adjectives and prepositions through educational and language programmes.

Nouns - common and proper nouns dealt with in phonics lessons, games of 'I-spy' etc.
Verbs - attention given to 'doing words' in games such as 'Simon Says' and during PE.
Prepositions - attention given through spatial awareness, using physical activities including stories, play, toys and imitating.
Adjectives - particularly during science and maths in relation to materials, eg shiny, smooth, heavy, light, colours etc. Also stressed in games such as 'Kim's Game'.

6. Literacy 'Hour'

It is generally felt that any child capable of accessing grammar at a higher level or who could totally cope with the Literacy Hour as directed by the National Strategy would be included in the mainstream class for that hour as part of their inclusion programme.

Children in the unit work in small groups to carry out designated activities or in a larger group for shared text activities. The level of need in the unit directs that few children work totally independently, as they generally require differentiated support to interpret the task set.

7. Assessment

In line with the assessment policy, children's work and success is assessed both formally and informally. Annually, at the time of the annual review, daybooks, record books and work are reviewed by the Head of Unit. Formal language assessment using the Derbyshire Language Scheme is carried out where appropriate. Termly discussion to focus staff upon a child's current needs adds to this assessment. Informally, note is taken of success levels and support required for a child to complete work.

8. Targeting

Formal targets are set for each child, along with Programmes of Study, following the annual review. Specific literacy targets are set for each year group in line with DfEE directives. Individually each child's target is based upon the scheme devised by the SLD schools' consortium (see table below).

9. Conclusion

Literacy time in the Aspen Unit is seen as an opportunity to take a more in-depth look at literacy in general and to take stock of targeting and assessment records. Above all it is to ensure that all children are educated to the best of their ability.

Bridge & NC Level	Speaking & Listening	Reading	Writing
React B1a	Able to identify sounds/movements/ gestures the pupil makes, that have the potential to be used as communication.	Introduced to being physically and/or verbally helped to explore textures and 3D objects in order to build up a conceptual framework of them.	Introduced to being physically and/or verbally helped to make marks, eg using fingers, hands, brushes, sponges, computer mouse or touch screen.
B1b	Occasionally reacts with sounds/movements/gestures to a stimulus or interaction with an adult which show like/dislike.	Tolerates being helped to explore textures and 3D objects sometimes.	Tolerates being helped to co-actively make marks in a variety of ways sometimes.
B1c	Able to show a consistent reaction to a stimulus, which can be taken to mean like/dislike. Reacts to interactions with an adult - makes eye contact or smiles when spoken to.	Tolerates being helped to explore a range of textures and 3D objects.	Tolerates being helped to make marks co-actively in a variety of ways on a variety of surfaces.
Anticipate B2a	Indicates an awareness of a link between actions or objects and an event, eg opens mouth/reaches out for a drink when sees a drink. May show a negative gesture or response.	Shows a visual/tactile interest in their surroundings or objects/textures presented.	Indicates an awareness of being helped to make marks, eg will look at their hands as helped to move them in the sand on a table.

Appendix 1

Bridge & NC Level		Speaking & Listening	Reading	Writing
	B2b	Indicates a consistent positive or negative response to familiar objects or events.	Sometimes shows the same positive/negative response to a 3D representation of an activity (obj. of ref.) as to the activity itself.	Shows a visual/tactile interest in the marks they have made co-actively or independently.
	B2c	Able to make choice between two things - eye pointing, gesture. Responds to simple commands given by a familiar person with situational clues - move arm towards coat sleeve when asked by adult holding coat ready.	Understands that objects of reference can carry meaning, ie consistently shows same response as to activity itself. Shows a consistent interest in 2D materials, eg will hold eye contact on a book/photo for short periods, eg 5 secs.	Understands that the marks they have made co-actively or independently are made by 'me'.
Initiate	B3a	Understands at a 1-word level (DLS) using real objects. Able to initiate communications by eye pointing or gesture at something wanted that is visible.	Beginning to understand that 2D representations of objects carry meaning, eg matches at least 2 familiar objects to 2D rep, from a choice of at least 2. Attends during the reading of a simple story.	Receptive to the idea that their work can be given meaning - smiles agrees etc. Able to 'label' their work with a given 2D rep, eg photo of their home. Able to 'map' left to right between 2 pictures.
	B3b	Understands at a 1-word level in generalised situations and 2-word level in routine situations. Understands that a spoken word/symbol/sign etc. can be used to communicate in structured situations, eg drinks time.	Able to 'read' at least 5 single symbols. Recognises the function of a book, eg will handle and turn the pages correctly and/or will show anticipation when a book is brought out to read.	Ascribes meaning to their work when given a choice of options either verbally or with symbols. Able to track L-R between 2 curved lines. (Max 2cm apart).
	B3c	Understands at a 2-word level in generalised situations. Able to communicate at a 1-word level using chosen system, eg speech, sign, symbols in generalised situations.	Able to read short phrases/sentences written in symbols. Enjoys book/stories, able to show preferences for favourites and respond to certain elements, eg begin/end or repetition.	Able to give meaning to their work whether painting/printing etc. or scribbled writing. Able to select symbols to describe an event/picture as lasting record. Able to overwrite letters 2cm high.
NC Level 1	L1.1	Understands at a 3-word level. Able to link 2 words/symbols/signs together with simple expressive phrases. Able to participate as both a speaker and a listener in structured group activities.	Understand that print is used to carry meaning in books and in everyday world. Recognises individual words/letters in familiar contexts, eg own name on coat peg.	Able to create images that carry meaning for other people. Able to independently write own name legibly or type with keyboard.
	L1.2	Understands at a 4-word level. Able to link 2 words/symbols/signs together with simple expressive phrases. Able to use both speaking and listening skills in a variety of situations, eg taking and receiving simple messages.	Able to retell elements of a simple, structured story, eg Billy Goats Gruff. Have a sight vocab of at least 10 words in generalised context.	Able to make attempt at labelling - some phonic awareness. Able to make legible written attempt to copy letters or has a working knowledge of a keyboard.
	L1.3	Understands at a 4+ word level. Able to communicate on matters of immediate interests or convey meanings with some detail, to a range of listeners using a recognised and clearly understood system.	Able to recognise familiar words in simple texts. Establishing a knowledge of a range of sounds and beginning to use these to read stories. Able to identify aspects of poem/stories they like.	Able to communicate meaning through simple words and phrases either written or typed by themselves or compiled by themselves. If writing, letters are clearly shaped and correctly orientated.

Bridge & NC Level	Speaking & Listening	Reading	Writing
NC Level 2 L2.1	Understands and uses simple structured sentences to receive and give information on matters of immediate interest. Demonstrates awareness that responses might be required in a dialogue. Listens with increased interest to spoken language where the topics interest.	Able to recognise and demonstrate understandings of familiar words out of context. Able to respond to major events in stories etc. Increasing knowledge of phonics and using this in word building.	Able to construct meaningful sentences developing a wider vocabulary. Able to spell some simple key words, eg mum, dad. Awareness of capital letters and the use of full stops. Able to form letters clearly from memory. Demonstrating some awareness of shape, size and spacing of letters.
L2.2	Shows awareness of the needs of the listener by beginning to make appropriate responses, including relevant detail in a dialogue. Listens with increased interest to a wider range of spoken language - stories, conversation and rhymes. Developing confidence in communicating with less familiar people.		
L2.3	Able to develop and explain own ideas using a growing vocabulary. Listens carefully and consistently. Responds appropriately in dialogue. Beginning to be aware that in some situations a more formal vocabulary and tone of voice are used.	Increasing accuracy and understanding of simple texts. Beginning to show understanding of main points of story. Make consistent use of more than one strategy when reading unfamiliar words.	Extend the range of writing forms. Showing awareness that writing is for different purposes and different readers. Some use of capital letters and full stops using various strategies. Attempting to spell unfamiliar and polysyllabic words. Beginning to adopt a cursive style of handwriting.
NC Level 3 L3.1	Talks and listens with some confidence in limited range of contexts. Actively participates in a discussion with some adjustments of language content for listener. Able to speak appropriately in a fomal context.	Read a range of texts with increasing fluency and accuracy. They are starting to read independently using a variety of strategies to establish meaning. Shows some understanding of main points and begins to express preferences. Awareness of alphabetical order to help find books and locate information.	Writing can be organised, imaginative and clear. Different forms used with awareness of reader. Sequences of sentences sometimes extend logically and words chosen for variety and interest. Sentences can reflect a basic grammatical structure. Key words spelt correctly, frequent use of punctuation and handwriting cursive.
L3.2	Talks and listens confidently in different contexts, exploring and communicating ideas. In discussion shows understanding of main points. Through relevant comments and questions shows have listened carefully. Adapts to the needs of listener, varying the use of vocabulary and level of detail. Begins to be aware of standard English.	Reads a range fluently and accurately. Reads independently using strategies appropriate to established meaning. Responds to fiction/non-fiction showing understanding of main points and preferences. Uses knowledge of alphabetical order to help find books and locate information.	Writing is often organised, imaginative and clear. Main features of different forms are used appropriately, beginning to be adapted to different readers. Sequences of sentences extend ideas logically and words are chosen for variety and interest. Basic grammatical structure of sentences and spelling are usually correct. Punctuation to make sentences - full stops, capital letters and question marks. Handwriting joined up and legible.
L3.3	Talks and listens with confidence in a range of contexts. In discussion shows clear understanding of main points. Comments and questions show increasing perception of others' ideas and views. Increased adaptation of language and vocab for needs of listener. Awarenesss of standard English.	Reads independently a wide range of texts and with increasing confidence. Shows clear understanding of the main points and expresses preferences in detail. Uses knowledge of alphabet competently.	Handwriting is usually organised, imaginative and clear. Main features of different forms of writing are adapted appropriately to different readers. Sequencing of sentences extend fluently and logically. A wide range of words chosen for deliberate effect. Grammatical structure is correct with accurate spelling.

Ref: Taken from ideas developed by Kent SLD Literacy consortium and Crossing The Bridge.

Journeys through the Literacy Hour with Key Stage 3

A. Holdsworth

Setting

Tor View School is an all age, 4-19, special school with one hundred pupils on roll. Pupils have a wide range of learning difficulties from Profound and Multiple Learning Difficulties (PMLD) through Severe Learning Difficulties (SLD) to Moderate Learning Difficulties (MLD). An increasing number of pupils exhibit challenging behaviour in addition to their learning difficulties.

The school is divided into three separate departments, Primary, Secondary and Further Education (FE) and liaison between departments is significant. The Primary Department consists of five mixed-ability classes vertically grouped according to the age of pupils. The Secondary Department also has five mixed-ability form groups. However, in the Secondary Department pupils are streamed into three teaching groups and taught by subject specialists. The 'Core group' is a small group of pupils with PMLD. Group 3(ii) are a group of pupils with SLD often with additional communication and sensory impairments. Group 3(i) are the most able pupils with moderate to severe learning difficulties. Pupils remain in Key Stage 3 for three years and therefore schemes of work operate on a three-year cycle.

The Headteacher is a considerable innovator and both he and the Senior Management team are highly supportive of new initiatives. I hold the post of Secondary Literacy/English Co-ordinator, a position supported by my counterpart and confidante in Primary.

Action

Following the *National Literacy Strategy* training in July 1998 a working party was established to implement the strategy in our setting. Members of the working party were the Literacy Governor, the Headteacher and the Primary and Secondary Literacy Co-ordinators. The outcome of the working party was the development of an Action Plan and a commitment to the adoption of a daily Literacy Hour for all pupils in Key Stages 1-3.

This article deals with the implementation of the Literacy Hour in Key Stage 3 since this is an area where matching the National Curriculum range to pupils' levels of interest and ability has been most challenging. The article also reflects more recent actions taken to respond to the *National Literacy Strategy* for Key Stage 3.

Starting point

Prior to the *National Literacy Strategy*, in order to develop a scheme of work for English which allowed age-appropriate progression and met individual needs, I had adopted a two-stranded approach, skill-based and content-based. The skill-based scheme of work lists English skills in a hierarchy starting with early development through to National Curriculum Level 3. It draws upon published and unpublished checklists and is currently being modified to incorporate the DfEE/QCA 'P' levels.

The existing content-based scheme of work for English reflected the range of statements from the then current National Curriculum and included age-appropriate set texts, for example, *Macbeth*, *The Canterbury Tales* and *A Christmas Carol* plotted on a three-year cycle. Figure 1 gives an outline mapping of the theme and main texts covered.

The challenge then was to marry this with the *National Literacy Strategy* framework and present pupils with a series of meaningful whole class experiences, involving multi-sensory teaching, which would enhance individual skills.

KS 3	AUTUMN	SPRING	SUMMER
Year 1 of cycle	**Food** - Contemporary poetry - Rosen, McGough etc.	**Travel** - *The Canterbury Tales* - Chaucer.	**Treasure** - *Treasure Island* - Louis Stephenson.
Year 2 of cycle	**Holidays** - *Our Day Out* - Russell.	**Imagination & Mystery** - Poetry pre-1900.	**News** - Contemporary poetry/poems from other cultures.
Year 3 of cycle	**Seasons** - *A Christmas Carol* - Dickens.	**Witches, Ghosts etc.** - *Macbeth* - Shakespeare.	**Animals** - *Cats* - Elliot, *Dirty Beasts* - Dahl.

Figure 1: Themes and texts.

Restructuring the Hour

Our working party had accepted that the Literacy Hour clock represented a good lesson plan, with opportunities for whole-class and individual work. In structuring our own Literacy Hour we were committed to maintaining a similar lesson format.

For the 3(i) and 3(ii) groups the 30 minutes of whole-class time for text, sentences and word level work was maintained but the teaching of signs, symbols and other communication/speech and language therapy targets were also included. In order to meet the needs of the groups, termly meetings were set up with the Speech and Language Therapist to clarify group and individual objectives.

The group/independent task time was replaced by individual/paired IEP or Target Work led by the teacher or a qualified Nursery Nurse (Special Support Assistant, Grade 3) and a group comprehension activity led by a Special Support Assistant (Grade 1). Derbyshire Language Scheme activities and other SSA 3-led structured programmes were included in Target Work time. This time was timetabled to ensure that the teacher taught each pupil every week. Where possible modifications were made to incorporate the literacy theme in target work. (This is illustrated later in this article.)

Finally, a short five-minute plenary was also included to allow the group working on the comprehension task to feedback and also to celebrate pupils' achievement of individual targets.

The Core group worked on a modified Hour with text and related group sensory experiences lasting for 15 to 20 minutes and greater emphasis being placed on individual communication targets.

Planning and delivery

My starting point was to familiarise myself with the *National Literacy Strategy* document. Our training informed us that the framework adopts a progressive two-year cycle. It seemed most appropriate therefore to consider the skill level of our most able pupils and match text level work from the *National Literacy Strategy*. A suitable match appeared to be at Year 3. Using the range of texts from the National Curriculum for Key Stage 3, I was able to modify the range of statements from the *National Literacy Strategy* framework and allocate appropriate text level work, ie group comprehension and composition, for each term.

For example, Term 1 of my scheme of work covered the work of the contemporary poets, Michael Rosen and Roger McGough. I had also chosen the theme of Food. I found a reasonable match with the fiction range for Year 3 Term 1, 'Stories with familiar setting; plays; poems based on observation and the senses and shape poems'. Indeed, by making reference to the *National Literacy Strategy* framework, I included additional materials, for example extracts from the musical *Oliver* and from Dickens' *Oliver Twist*.

Planning for the 3(ii) and for the Core group grew from my planning for the more able pupils. In order to give them the same curriculum entitlement, the same range and in most cases the same texts were offered. The texts were supported by the provision of props, Makaton signs, symbols, role-play etc. to ensure that the experience was meaningful. The food theme gave plenty of opportunities for sensory work. The simple poem 'yellow butter, purple jelly, red jam, black bread' provided contrasts of taste, texture and smell, and appropriate language was reinforced by single-word phrases recorded onto the 'Big Mack' communication aids. Non-fiction texts included reading and following instructions on jelly and instant custard packets. Poetry included rhyming words, for example 'mustard' and 'custard', but also reflected individual needs, from making a choice about what would be eaten, through phonological awareness to onset and rime and spelling families.

The theme lasted a term and was a huge success. The SSA staff were extremely resourceful and creative providing props, rehearsing signs, dressing up etc. The purchase of a school laminator, literacy OHP, scanner and digital camera coupled with the PC version of the 'Writing with Symbols' program, allowed us to produce some high-quality resources which can be reused in future years.

Following the enormous success of the first term's work I was concerned that we would not be able to maintain our initial momentum and enthusiasm. This was a particular concern since our second term's theme was Travel and I had chosen the more demanding *Canterbury Tales* and *The Highway Code*. Again I referred to the *National Literacy Strategy* framework to identify some related text level work that would challenge the most able pupils. A reasonable match was found with the fiction range for Year 3 Term 2, 'Myths, legends, fables, parables, traditional stories, stories with related themes; oral and performance poetry from other cultures'.

As before I found the structure of the *National Literacy Strategy* to be helpful, since the references to character portraits in the text level work led easily into the use of pictures, photographs and symbols for the less able pupils. Storyboards were used at all levels from sentence work using a 'Wordhunter' dictionary to sequencing and role-play using symbols and finger puppets. With the support of my SSAs we were able to condense each of the tales into four simple sentences and create picture sequencing activities which reflected the pupils' speech and language therapy targets. For example, *The Miller's Tale* became:

1. Nicholas loved Alison.
2. John went in the barrel.
3. Nicholas and Alison went to bed.
4. Nicholas got a burnt bottom.

The picture sequencing tasks were offered at two levels with some children sequencing the pictures and matching the text in response to the story. A simplified version was keyword matching where pupils were given one or two keywords from the sentences and asked to select the correct picture.

On a more simplistic level *The Nun's Priest's Tale* was a wonderful opportunity to reinforce Makaton animal signs without revisiting the less age-appropriate and over-familiar 'Old MacDonald'. Indeed, using a fox glove puppet, one of the pupils learnt eight new body parts and thereby attained an individual target. The SSA was inspired by the act of the fox grabbing Chanticleer by the neck.

Parent helpers were increasingly involved since our *National Literacy Strategy* action plan included running parents' workshops to inform and include parents. Contributions have been varied such as taping extracts from different versions of the tales, producing resources to be used in class and actively joining literacy sessions in school. We have already decided that on our revisit to *The Canterbury Tales* in two years we will embark on our own pilgrimage, a visit to a local church, telling tales and singing songs on the way.

The summer term's theme was Treasure and the Literacy Hour format was becoming well established. Following the successful practice of our Primary Department, which starts each session with a rhyme or song, we started each session with 'Fifteen men on a dead man's chest...' sung to the tune of 'What shall we do with the drunken sailor' and supported by Makaton signs. Planning made use of Year 3 Term 3 of the *National Literacy Strategy* framework 'Adventure and mystery stories'. The more able pupils covered the appropriate learning objectives including first and third person accounts, character studies etc.

Medium Term planning used the 'Half Termly Planner' from the *National Literacy Strategy* Framework document. Figures 2 and 3 show how differentiation from the 3(i) and 3(ii) groups was built into the process.

Class: 3(i)	Year Group(s): KS3	Year: 9 8-99	Term: Summer 1st Half	Teacher: A. Holdsworth

Phonics, Spelling & Vocabulary	Grammar & Punctuation	Comprehension & Composition	Texts
Continuous work:	Continuous work:	Continuous work:	Range:
Develop independent spelling strategies, use of analogy, word hunter, look, say, trace, cover, write and check. Revision and consolidation of basic phonics; letter sounds, names, blends and syllables. Read and spell key words.	Demonstrating use of grammatical knowledge. Capital letters, full stops, commas and speech marks. Deletion and substitution activities. Identification of pronouns.	Sequencing main events. Evaluate and justify opinions. Character study - emotions, behaviour etc. Read aloud/recite poetry.	Adventure and mystery stories; stories by the same author, humorous poetry, poetry that plays with language, word puzzles, puns and riddles.
Blocked work:	Blocked work:	Blocked work:	Titles:
Identification of keywords in news writing.	Capital letters for names and places. Use of pronoun I.	Own news. Recount of events from holidays. Use of news writing frame. First and third person accounts.	News.
Spelling 'ew' family words (p, d, n, f, m) and (cr, br, dr, st, fl). Rhyming words in song lyrics.	Substitution of adjectives - character descriptions.	Sequencing main events. Character descriptions.	The Sea Chest.
Spelling 'um' family words (r, b, g, h, s) and (j-p, b-p, d-p, h-p, l-p).	Substitution of adjectives - character descriptions.	Character descriptions - emotive and reasons for behaviours. Succinctly conveying meaning. Writing for a known audience.	The Voyage.
Spelling 'en' and 'est' families (m, t, d, h, p) and (ch, r, p, b, n).	Identification/understanding of pronouns in the text.	Understanding/sequencing of events.	Message in a bottle.
Phonological awareness - rhyming words.	Adjectives - descriptive use of.	Sea poetry.	Sea Poems.
Spelling family revision.	Capital letters for names and places. Use of pronoun I.	Recall sequence of events, concurrent events.	News.
Revision of spelling families. Letter name and sound work from text.	Adjectives to create excitement and tension.	Character descriptions - emotions and reasons for behaviours.	My Shore. Adventure Begins.

Figure 2: National Literacy Strategy - Medium Term Planning Half-termly Planner: Group 3(i).

Tasks were presented to the less able pupils using picture description and sequencing tasks. Learning prepositions 'in', 'on' and 'under' were IEP targets for a number of pupils. Therefore, structured Derbyshire Language Scheme tasks were modified and made more relevant and age-appropriate by replacing the traditional 'Dolly' and 'Teddy' with a treasure item and giving pupils commands to put the ring, bracelet or coin 'in', 'on' and 'under' the box as appropriate. Symbol cards were also produced so that appropriate expression could be elicited, allowing pupils to meet early speaking and listening targets.

Group 3(i) increasingly became a resource for 3(ii) since, through shared writing, the 3(i) group would précis more complex texts which then became accessible to the less able group. This was a mutually beneficial activity since it not only gave 3(i) a purpose for their writing but also led to greater enthusiasm from the 3(ii) group as texts could be personalised with references made to individuals or shared experiences. To maintain the seafaring theme and give novelty some of the written pieces were placed in a bottle, flavoured with rum essence and presented as 'messages in a bottle'. The 'special' rum-scented paper sparked increased response from all the pupils.

Class: 3(ii)	Year Group(s): KS3	Year: 9 8-99	Term: Summer 1st Half	Teacher: A. Holdsworth

Phonics, Spelling & Vocabulary	Grammar & Punctuation	Comprehension & Composition	Texts
Continuous work:	Continuous work:	Continuous work:	Range:
Develop phonological awareness. Revision and consolidation of letter sounds and names. Identifying, matching and reading keywords. 'Treasure' signs and symbols.	Capital and lower case letters.	Sequencing main events. Make choices. Character study good/bad etc. Recognition of Makaton signs and symbols. Contribution to shared writing.	Adventure and mystery stories; stories by the same author, humorous poetry, poetry that plays with language, word puzzles, puns and riddles.
Blocked work:	Blocked work:	Blocked work:	Titles:
Keywords. Use of writing with symbols.	Capital letters, own name, I and first initial.	Own news. Recount of event.	News.
Understanding of treasure and island.	Negatives/absence.	Sequencing. Character descriptions.	The Sea Chest.
Signs and initial letter sound work using objects (s, a, r, p, b, c, m).	We took ...	Sequencing of main events. Character descriptions.	The Voyage.
Signs and initial letter sound work using objects (s, a, r, p, b, c, m).	I need ...	Understanding/sequencing of events.	Message in a bottle.
Signs and initial sound work using seaside resources (s, t, h).	Lists. Descriptive adjectives.	Sensory poetry.	Sea Poems.
Signs and initial sounds work (M, T, W, F, S).	We... Days of week.	Sequence of events. Diary writing.	News.
Signs and initial sounds work using objects (t, w, s, g, l, c, b).	I saw...	Sequencing of main events. Character descriptions.	My Shore. Adventure Begins.

Figure 3: Medium Term Planning Half-termly Planner: Group 3(ii).

A visit from the schools' SEN Advisor in the summer term was extremely positive with praise for all the staff involved. The climax was a legitimate English Curriculum trip to the seaside at the end of term and an opportunity to wear bandannas and bury and dig for treasure.

Key Stage 3 Literacy Strategy

The launch of the Key Stage 3 Literacy Strategy and subsequent training caused us to consider the wider application of literacy throughout the Secondary Department. The two-day training had outlined successful projects in a number of pilot schools and drawn out the features to which the success was attributed. Of these, most significant appeared to be a supportive Senior Management Team and a commitment to a series of initiatives making a multi-faceted approach. The support of the SMT had never been an issue. In addition to the adoption of the Literacy Hour for Key Stage 3 in September 1998 we had also introduced a more structured approach to 'Reading in form time' and provided staff literacy training for subject specialists in Key Stages 3 and 4.

The 'Reading in form time' was an initiative to promote reading in the Secondary Department. A new Secondary Library was opened and staffed by parent helpers, for forms to use during morning registration. In light of the success of the Primary Department, which encourages home-school reading through the use of reading diary and green book bag, all secondary pupils were given a black duffel bag for their reading/library books and a modified reading diary. The diaries and reading materials were developed by the English Department. The diary listed pupils' individual reading targets. These ranged from making eye contact with pages in the book, page turning, finding keywords in the text to reading with increased fluency and expression. Training was provided for form teachers during school development plan time and parents were involved through two reading workshops. An ongoing monitoring programme was established, involving SMT observations of form-time and a close observation of entries made in reading diaries by the secondary English teachers.

The need for literacy awareness training for subject specialists was identified by our schools *National Literacy Strategy* Working Party. The recognition that the format of the Literacy Hour reflected a well-balanced lesson led us to suggest that subject specialists could adopt some of the teaching methods and the basic structure of the Hour in their lessons. Training sessions made use of the non-fiction section of the 'Literacy Lunchbox' and covered the use of enlarged texts, concept mapping and writing frames. A broad definition of literacy was again employed and the use of pictures, symbols and augmentative communication aids was also included. This training has had an impact in a number of departments, notably Food Technology where use has been made of symbol recipes and Science where brainstorming and shared writing are increasingly a feature of lessons.

Future

In response to the emphasis of cross-curricular literacy at Key Stage 3 we have set aside School Development Plan time and resources to further develop cross-curricular communication and literacy over the next two years. We have also enlisted the support of our school's Speech and Language Therapist to enhance this process.

Conclusions

The *National Literacy Strategy,* in both providing structure and allowing flexibility to meet the needs of individual pupils, has proved to be a useful resource and a stimulus for whole school development. In Tor View School:

- the teaching of literacy has been reviewed and enhanced;
- the experiences of the pupils have been enriched;

- the expectations of staff and pupils have been raised;
- the involvement of parents has been increased;
- the commitment of all staff to the development of literacy has been strengthened.

On a more personal level these journeys through the Literacy Hour have left me feeling more confident, enthusiastic and determined to build and expand upon the work already begun.

The Implementation of the National Literacy Strategy (NLS) in I CAN's Three Special Schools

David Braybrook

From September 1998, all primary schools were expected to implement the *National Literacy Strategy* (NLS) and in particular to introduce the Literacy Hour. Special schools were expected to implement the NLS as far as possible taking account of the needs of the pupils. The expectation was that literacy lessons in special schools should be as close as possible to those in mainstream primary schools.

Teachers in special schools were required to exercise their professional judgement and expertise to determine the extent to which it was appropriate to apply the structure of the framework document. They were not required to devote an uninterrupted hour a day to literacy, but to consider the use of the strategy depending on the needs of the pupils.

I CAN's three non-maintained special schools reviewed their literacy work in the light of the strategy and implemented a pilot literacy project across the last school year. The three schools, Meath, John Horniman and Dawn House reviewed their pilot work towards the end of the school year and evaluated its effectiveness in terms of outcomes, issues and concerns and used the information to inform their current work. The following summarises the evaluation work in the two primary and one all-age school for pupils with speech and language difficulties. Ms Maggi Hunt, Director of the Newcastle Literacy Collaborative, kindly agreed to act as Literacy Consultant for the pilot. She was involved in accessing how well the schools modified and adapted the NLS to meet the needs of the pupils, many of whom have complex speech and language needs, and to consider the overall effectiveness of the project.

Meath School

The school has been piloting the use of the *National Literacy Strategy* since October 1998. Class timetables were scrutinised in autumn 1998 to assess the range of literacy teaching and staff attended INSET training to familiarise themselves with the key components of the framework. A more comprehensive review of the literacy curriculum was conducted in spring 1999, with staff mapping current practice against the framework components.

Pilot projects had already been highlighted from the first audit. Our aims were to:

- determine the viability of using the framework with speech and language impaired pupils;
- assess the impact of a shared reading and writing focus on text level components of the strategy;
- assess the use of shared text for focused word and sentence work.

Two classes of Year 5 and Year 6 and 7 pupils began the pilot project in October 1998, with a third class of Year 4 and 5 pupils entering the project in January 1999. The three classes selected a group of up to six pupils whom they had identified as the most homogenous group in terms of their literacy skills. Each class conducted one or two sessions a week, varying in length from 30 minutes to an hour.

It was not possible to produce quantitative data on outcomes from the use of the framework because of the additional literacy activities in each class. The following evaluation is based on monitoring of planning and teaching and from discussion with staff and children.

Strengths and outcomes

- The NLS provides a comprehensive framework for Individual Education Plans (IEP) targets and curriculum planning and teaching, although objectives often need to be more finely graded to show attainment and progress.
- Shared reading focused the pupil's attention towards the book and the adult. Optimal use could be made of Paget Gorman Signed Speech to cue word recognition and highlight syntactic elements. The adult could also use Cued Articulation to the group to develop phonological skills at word level.
- The pupils were introduced to a wider range of genres in shared reading and the adult could support their exploration of the genre through discussion and shared writing.
- Shared writing reduced the enormity of the task of writing individually and increased the pupil's willingness to make a contribution.
- There was a positive effect on group dynamics, with a sense of shared achievement in writing sessions. Adults noted an improvement in most of the pupils' attention and response to each other.

Constraints and issues

- Staff were concerned whether the pupils' individual literacy needs can be met using the framework. There needs to be a balance between whole class literacy sessions and specific literacy teaching and therapy during the week. Staff involved in the pilot projects acknowledged that one or two literacy sessions weekly were insufficient. From September 1999 all classes have had three class literacy sessions weekly and additional literacy activities will continue outside these sessions.
- There are issues to be resolved regarding pupils being taken out of literacy sessions for therapy. Most classes will initially use all staff to implement the sessions and therapists will monitor the effect this has on meeting individual therapy targets.
- Most pupils have a baseline entry to the framework at several years below their chronological year group and have an uneven profile across the three components of the framework. Information collated on each pupil's profile will be used to plan for group teaching, either at the initial shared stage of the session or for word or sentence level work at the next stage.
- Staff felt they would need to be flexible about the timing of the different elements of the session and the overall length of the session.
- There is a difficulty in finding enough appropriate text to achieve text level objectives. Time will need to be allocated to modifying text and collating resources to support the text.
- Additional planning time for literacy by the class team will need to be allocated.

During the Autumn Term 1999 the curriculum co-ordinator and the headteacher monitored the planning and delivery of the literacy sessions. INSET continued on different components of the *National Literacy Strategy* and the curriculum co-ordinator was available to work with class teams either for planning or during the sessions. There was a review in December 1999.

John Horniman School

As with all DfEE initiatives, the school has spent time evaluating the *National Literacy Strategy* from the perspective of a special school for children with speech and language difficulties. The following outline of **strengths** and **concerns** indicates why modifications were made, whilst still meeting the requirements of the NLS and addressing the Statemented needs of all pupils at the school.

The termly objectives prescribed in the document
Strengths
- Teaching staff acknowledge that coverage of literacy has broadened since working from the *National Literacy Strategy,* eg a wider range of material used with more of a focus on the text.
- Teaching staff acknowledge that the strategy provides a far more realistic basis for detailed planning than the National Curriculum terminology.
- The strategy format has provided a framework for uniformity and consistency of teaching and in evaluating progress throughout the school and for each pupil.

Concerns
- The *National Literacy Strategy* was devised for the mainstream school environment. Pupils with specific speech, language and communication impairment also have significant difficulties with literacy, therefore their needs are often very different to those of most mainstream pupils.

Outcomes
- The school will follow the content of the *National Literacy Strategy* document. However, teachers' planning will be led by the specific needs of each pupil rather than the sequence and pace of the integrated termly objectives of the NLS.
- The termly objectives for word, sentence and text level will be broken down into smaller steps to allow for meaningful planning and target setting.
- Texts should be relevant to the needs of the pupils. For example, in the school's lowest language comprehension group the daily activities strip is the only text used; this menu of the events of the day forms the basis of literacy teaching every day as it uses words and events that are significant and meaningful.
- Teachers' curriculum plans will indicate word, sentence and text level objectives.
- Weekly plans will detail literacy teaching to provide a basis for collaborative interdisciplinary working.
- IEPs will include the *National Literacy Strategy* objectives and progress against these monitored to inform future planning.
- Evidence of word, sentence and text level work will be included in children's individual portfolios each term.
- Teachers will use the *National Literacy Strategy* word lists to chart each pupil's literacy progress.

The Hour format
Strengths
- The whole class focus on a common text has met with some success in that it has widened the range of text used and provided a starting point for individual or group work.

Concerns
- With pupils being taken out for therapy, it was difficult to reserve a specific 'hour' every day; it was felt that pupils could not be taken out of a class literacy lesson unless it was an integral part of the literacy planning (which had a significant impact on Speech and Language Therapy treatment plans).
- The specific times in the 'hour' were considered to be too rigid, particularly for the diversity of skills within the class groups. Teachers saw the value of an initial class focus for some literacy teaching, but preferred to adapt the timing in order to maximise resources and learning.
- It was felt that some literacy work was better accessed only in small groups or individually.
- Speaking and listening appears to have been overlooked as an essential prerequisite to literacy.

Outcomes

- Teachers deliver literacy programmes to best meet the needs of the pupils in a class group, ie some lessons will follow class/group/plenary procedure, while others will be delivered in small groups/individually.
- Teachers are flexible in their timetabling of literacy lessons to maximise use of key-workers and resources.
- Teachers and therapists establish a minimum of one session each week of collaborative working in literacy.
- Although the school is not timetabling the Literacy Hour, the Hour still has a high profile and will be timetabled for between 5.5 and 6.5 hours per week per class.
- Speaking and listening are featured separately on the timetables.

Conclusion

The school has recognised the prescriptive objectives of the document, but has modified them both in terms of pace and sequence in order to meet the specific learning needs of our pupils. The multi-disciplinary environment along with the diversity of attention and literacy skills in each class group has shown that the implementation of the 'hour' is not necessarily as effective as other formats. We continue to teach literacy in a highly structured, intensive way yet using a variety of approaches.

Dawn House

After a term of careful planning, the Literacy Hour was introduced in September 1998. From the outset it was decided that the delivery of the Literacy Hour would follow the *National Literacy Strategy* as set out in the guidance. The school decided to use the framework as a starting point, whilst reviewing delivery from the beginning in order to tailor it to the needs of our pupils. The only change made to take account of their needs was that work at text, sentence and word level was at a stage below the chronological ages of the children involved.

Issues

Planning systems established in Summer 1998 involved core teams of teacher, speech and language therapist and classroom assistant and continued on a weekly basis throughout the year. Monitoring arrangements were put in place by the headteacher and initially concentrated on staff delivery and whole class response. Later monitoring by co-ordinators concentrated on individual pupil response. Progress was evaluated.

Pupils in all classes seemed to enjoy the structure and routine of the Literacy Hour, with younger children (Key Stage 1) participating particularly well in whole class sessions. Group work was rotated to ensure all pupils worked on the different skills being taught.

A baseline had been established by testing on the Neale Analysis of Reading and the use of the basic sight vocabulary reading and spelling lists within the strategy framework. A bank of resources and equipment is being continually updated, making planning and preparation less onerous. Loan material from Nottinghamshire County Council is used effectively alongside purchased materials.

Time and practice have demonstrated the need to adopt the structure of the framework to allow greater depth on fewer teaching points when working with pupils with speech, language and communication disorders.

The plenary session, first used for reporting back, now involves pupil evaluation of their own work in the two Key Stage 2 classes.

Strengths and outcomes

Pupil response, gathered by observation and core team evaluation sheets, was and still is very positive. Steady progress in listening skills, signing, using initial letter sounds and recognising sight vocabulary are clearly evident. The recent OfSTED inspection of the school identified the Literacy Hour as one of the strengths of a good school. It enables the pupils to make good progress in reading and writing. The report says that the introduction of the *National Literacy Strategy* has been very successful and is having a very good effect on the pupils' learning and that teaching in the Literacy Hour ranges from very good to excellent.

The Literacy Strategy is now in its second year. The whole class approach has made it easier to pick up on any distractibility and access problems relating to individual pupils, particularly with our excellent staff ratios.

Year 7 trialled the Literacy Strategy approach in the Summer Term with a good measure of success. September 1999 saw the extension of the Key Stage 3 trial into Year 8. Teachers and speech and language therapists are planning and implementing the Strategy together and have high expectations of continuing success. This is already being noted in improved concentration and the gradual acquisition of more age-appropriate reading, spelling, comprehension and general writing skills.

As with the Primary Department, baselines have been established, progress will be measured and other formative procedures used in a wide variety of written work tasks.

The introduction of the *National Literacy Strategy* has been very successful. Initially staff felt that it would not be an appropriate vehicle for teaching our pupils literacy skills. However, through the allocation of adequate time for liaison and planning, through drawing on the differing but complementary skills of our multidisciplinary team and building in time for review and evaluation, the *National Literacy Strategy* has helped to raise the levels of literacy in our pupils. Staff now feel that the strategy had enabled them to reappraise the way that they teach literacy skills, to introduce pupils to a wider variety of genres and develop their literacy skills across the curriculum.

PART TWO: MAINSTREAM SCHOOLS
Primary Schools and the Hour: 'Lunacy Hour or Luxury Hour?'

Dorothy Smith

Most responses were received from this sector as one would expect. Twenty-four schools sent in quite detailed pro formas. Three were from separate infants schools, one from the teacher of an Area Support Centre attached to a mainstream middle school and one from the SENCO in a 9-13 middle school. They were from large schools, the largest being a junior school of 820 pupils and 24 classes, and from smaller schools (two schools with 230 pupils and a separate infants school with 180 on roll). But it appeared that no school of less than 100 pupils sent in a response. Not all gave their pupil numbers. Some were described as being on a 'culturally diverse estate', as being 'urban', as being 'suburban', as being 'deprived', from a 'council estate' and a 'village' school. Thus a full range of schools is being described. One school of 300+ pupils mentioned that it had 100 pupils on its Special Needs Register.

Most respondents were Special Educational Needs Co-ordinators, a few were support teachers and most had other responsibilities within the school. Some were headteachers, some were class teachers and some were literacy co-ordinators. One return was a collective set of staff views. All seemed very honest when responding, with one school mentioning that it was nearly into special measures a year or two back and the new headteacher had been appointed to cope with this. The subtitle for this section is a quote from one headteacher who was positive about the Literacy Hour but who recognised its many difficulties.

Pupils with special educational needs and their particular problems in coping with the Hour

Schools contained a wide variety of children with special educational needs. As would be expected the main categories mentioned were moderate learning difficulties, specific learning difficulties and speech and language problems. Emotional and behavioural difficulties featured in many of the responses and the words 'lack of concentration' were used frequently. It was also frequently noted that children with weak reading abilities had problems with accessing texts independently. Occasionally schools described more specialised problems such as Down's syndrome, dyspraxia, autistic spectrum disorder and Asperger's syndrome, sensory impairments and cerebral palsy. Schools constantly noted the low self-esteem which was prevalent amongst these children.

Some particulars
- One infants school described its pupils as having a high level of language and learning difficulties. There are 40% of pupils with English as an Additional Language on the EMAG register and there are others with emotional and behavioural difficulties. This school's LEA has a policy of inclusion which adds quite complex problems but the children are allocated varying degrees of Learning Support Assistant support (usually one or two hours per week).
- One of the urban schools has nine children with Statements (eight with 'global delay' and one with emotional and behavioural difficulties). 26% of the school population is on the Special Needs Register.
- 28 pupils in a large junior school have Statements within six categories.
- Another junior school mentioned no pupils with Statements but wrote that the Stage 3 children tended to have specific literacy difficulties or phonological awareness problems, speech and language problems and moderate learning difficulties.
- The literacy set of 26 pupils taught by the SENCO in a junior school of 300 pupils contained no pupils with Statements but there were four pupils placed at Stage 3, six at Stage 2, four at Stage 1 with one pupil having mild cerebral palsy.

- Pupils with special educational needs in the middle school with the ASC (Area Support Centre) were reported usually to have reading accuracy ages of below 8 years, comprehension ages of between 7 and 9 years and spelling ages below 8 years. All of these were placed on Stages 2 or 3 or had Statements. All pupils in the unit had Statements. Pupils with specific learning difficulties are also included in the withdrawal groups to help their self-esteem and confidence. (This differs from one response which pointed out that a pupil with dyslexia hated being withdrawn for literacy support.)

Most of the schools outlined the problems they experienced when having to organise the Literacy Hour for the numbers of children with special educational needs and the range of problems presented. Schools felt that at times there were difficulties achieving the individual targets planned for pupils. Differentiation of some parts of the Literacy Hour posed problems especially for pupils in Years 5 and 6. Because some of the respondents were support teachers or SENCOs who worked part-time with the Literacy Hour, they mentioned the difficulties they experienced when coping with timetabling. They were not always able to work with the pupils on a daily basis and couldn't work with as many pupils who they felt needed help. Helping the individual on a regular basis was also mentioned as a particular problem and additional literacy teaching and support had to be presented at other times during the week. There was also mention of lack of time for organisation and collaboration between adults who supported and ran the literacy work. As in the previous book and as in the secondary and special school responses, poor concentration skills were one of the most worrying aspects of certain pupils finding it hard to access the Literacy Hour.

Some particulars
- Poor concentration and low levels of language acquisition on admission to school were found to be a problem in an infants school. The staff had to overcome the fact that some children had minimal home support and it was also noted that differentiation of work was very difficult.
- Even within small groups a wide range of abilities was noted which caused initial difficulties in particular with finding appropriate material. Middle school pupils needed work that didn't appear to be too 'babyish'. This school queried whether pupils with dyslexia were really being catered for but felt that one autistic pupil gained a great deal from the structure of the *National Literacy Strategy.*
- Because of 'inclusion' issues and whole class teaching, one school found that satisfactory timetabling (eg for dyslexic pupils) was almost impossible. Also the Literacy Hour work was not always at the correct level for particular pupils as the complex English grammar was too difficult for some.
- Social, emotional and behavioural problems were difficult to address within the structure of the Hour according to the response of a large primary school of over 300 pupils. Where setting or withdrawal was not possible due to staff shortage it was clear that children with special educational needs were severely disadvantaged by the pace of the Hour. The SENCO was assigned to provide Reading Recovery for selected pupils in Years 1 and 2 and to provide for other children with special educational needs at Stages 1-3 throughout the school. She also trained and co-ordinated parent volunteers in a successful parent partnership scheme.
- One primary school stated that because of its organisational set-up and the SENCO's hours children could miss parts of the Literacy Hour while withdrawn. It was also felt that texts for Year 6 were above the ability of pupils with special educational needs. The SENCO also reported that time for planning with the class teacher was not always available.
- 'Literacy Strategy abandoned by SENCO!' She worked on four or five activities in each session to reinforce the learning, using flashcards, tick lists, snap games, letter sounds for example. These were pupils in Years 3 and 4 who failed to gain a reading age on NFER reading tests.

- One primary school felt that the beginning and the plenary sessions of the Hour could be the most problematical because of their length of time and the pupils' problems with lack of concentration and ability to keep on task and also because of the differentiation needed. This school also encountered difficulties finding texts which were stimulating but academically appropriate for pupils at all levels of special educational need and initiating group activities which would promote independence.

Literacy Hour arrangements

It was difficult to summarise this section because schools showed a variety of ways of organisation. However, from the 24 returns:

- Thirteen mentioned that there was whole-class teaching for at least part of the Hour.
- Twelve mentioned that for part of the Hour there was some withdrawal of pupils, sometimes in groups or sometimes individually. One support teacher mentioned that she was pleased that she was still able to withdraw pupils. One SENCO felt that withdrawing a special needs group (although not all the pupils on the SEN register were withdrawn) has helped the other groups within the class.
- Eight mentioned the words setting or streaming and this seemed to be by ability with the lower or less able sets being smaller and taught by either support teachers, the SENCO or learning support assistants. Occasionally a school mentioned that the learning support assistants were 'qualified' but they didn't go into any details of what these qualifications might be.
- Eleven mentioned that the groups for independent work were supported by other adults (usually learning support assistants) and the groupings were either chosen by ability or by attainment.
- One school explained that there were some groups set for creative writing and spelling outside the Hour and that the SENCO withdrew one group twice a week during word level work for earlier phonic skills.

Some schools emphasised that their arrangements worked well because of the extra adults employed. For example, in one Scottish primary school three of the Primary 1 classes were given early literacy activities on three occasions a week for about 45 minutes a session. They were streamed and 11 adults were needed, comprising class teachers, the deputy headteacher, the learning support teacher, learning support assistants and parent helpers.

Apart from the Scottish schools all other returns showed that the format of the Hour was adhered to except for one school. This was a large junior school who before they had an OfSTED inspection had felt trapped by the Hour's format and believed themselves to be rigid in their approach. However, an inspector said 'children have needs' rather than requiring the dictates of the Literacy Hour and so the school changed to running three special educational needs groups in Years 3, 4 and 6 and in Year 5 there were five streamed groups. The weaker sets had 80% of the pupils with Statements of Special Educational Need.

Strategies to overcome problems

As can be imagined there were many suggestions and ideas in this section which showed the ingenuity and creativity of the staff involved and the depth of thought which went into planning the Literacy Hour for pupils with special educational needs.

Ideas included:

Organisation
- Running mini Literacy Hours parallel to the main class.

- Adapting the *National Literacy Strategy* components as appropriate (eg making 'carpet time' less long).
- Working on guided reading at separate times.
- Continuing of withdrawal for short periods several times a week in order to meet the needs of more complex difficulties (maybe contrary to advice but the school believes it's right).
- Putting children with SLD in an earlier year group for some of the literacy sessions.
- Following the *National Literacy Strategy* at a level lower than the child's actual age (eg take objectives from Year 1 and Reception such as the high frequency words).
- Being flexible with the timings within the Hour.
- Training of children to work independently.
- Consulting and involving pupils about their feelings about withdrawal/inclusion.
- Finding and using additional rooms.
- Delivering all literacy in the morning so children are not taken out of other lessons.
- Providing continuity for SEN children (same room, same teacher, same supporters).
- Making groups small (normally not over eight).
- Disapplying the Literacy Hour for certain children for specific periods of time so they can recover their self-esteem.
- Organising the timetable around the special needs timetable rather than vice versa.
- Supporting by working in classrooms as it is easier to feed children back in and relate work to what the rest of the class are doing.
- Organising small 'catch-up' groups during word level work.
- Key Stage 2 staff approval of pupils on the Code of Practice Stages 2 and 3 being withdrawn for one whole Literacy Hour where they might preview a class text or work more intensively on reading and writing strategies.

Programme of work
- Including phonological training as part of the group work activities.
- Acknowledging that some pupils may need their own individual programmes.
- Purchasing appropriate resources and making 'home-made' materials.
- Making appropriate use of videos, OHPs and simplified texts.
- Linking IEP objectives to the *National Literacy Strategy*.
- Tailoring the IEPs to the child's needs so that they can be given some independent tasks.
- Preparing of texts and discussing of questions likely to be asked in advance.
- Using pictograms for keywords.
- Integrating speech and language programmes into the sessions with appropriate support.
- Differentiating tasks and activities.
- Carefully assessing the strengths and weaknesses of individual children in order to inform teaching.
- Providing lots of oral work with differentiated questioning.
- Using word lists linked to age.

Adults involved
- Using Learning Support Assistants to take groups.
- Using other members of staff to split classes.
- Exchanging ideas with other members of staff.
- Undertaking a project to involve parents to raise awareness of the Literacy Hour.
- Organising a GNVQ group within the school so students can support in the Literacy Hour.
- Providing every class with an LSA during the Literacy Hour.
- Sitting support teacher near pupils to encourage participation.
- Using an LSA (City and Guilds trained) to 'teach' the ALS materials to Level 2c group.

- Appointing three extra NNEBs on a part-time basis to support pupils (and if finances cannot afford this then their learning suffers).
- Using 'extra hands' to make differentiated tasks during the Hour possible and meaningful.

Resource implications

Teachers were realistic in their thoughts about what they have found works and what they might need to make the Literacy Hours work more efficiently. As would be expected they asked for time, 'time and opportunity for differentiating tasks', 'time to manage resources', 'time for extended writing' and 'time for specific teaching around the mainstream curriculum'. Also they asked for other adults. 'To work at an optimal level all Literacy Hours need the support of a Learning Support Assistant' stated one writer. Others requested 'staffing to split groups', 'someone to develop and make materials' and 'without support the SEN pupils find they are floundering'. 'Adult support works - it is vital!' and 'People work' seem to sum up schools' sentiments.

Respondents showed concern about their own roles within their schools where special educational needs were concerned. One stated that the SENCO and the 'supporter' should be the same person and that class teachers should not become the SENCO each year as this doesn't help continuity. Another felt that SENCOs need to be experienced special needs practitioners whilst another said that learning support teachers' time must be protected and they should not be used as supply teachers. It was emphasised that all support needs to be flexible, involving as much joint planning and discussion as possible. This goes back to the need for time.

Few problems were mentioned and these were that:
- Group reading works but has enormous resource implications.
- Shared text in a mixed ability set-up is a nightmare.
- Older pupils become disaffected as they cannot follow the flow of the complex text which is selected to meet the objectives of stretching the average to able members of the class.
- There is pressure on using sets of books which means the pace of the lessons is not always appropriate.
- Most children with special educational needs are not at a level to work independently and when not withdrawn these children struggle with classwork as they require lots of props.
- There are difficulties in finding enlarged text for the shared session.
- Finding a range of appropriate texts and a variety of activities.

General suggestions and ideas were that:
- Mini-whiteboards are essential for the special needs groups.
- Replacing books every two to three years is necessary.
- The purchase of books which are appropriate in terms of readability and interest levels should be aimed for.
- Computers work. The school mentioning this supplied one for every 13 children although the writer would love more plus Dream Writer as a program.
- Spending money on books is important. (From £6000 spent half of this was raised by parents.)
- Big books are both popular and effective (especially if some pupils have an individual small copy).
- Practical resources such as games and magnetic letters are helpful.
- Multi-sensory approaches fit the Hour well (such as colours on a whiteboard, tactile letters, Language Masters and Listening Centres).
- Money for photocopying is important.
- An OHP for every group is helpful (but one respondent mentioned that children with learning difficulties find it hard to cope with reading from this).

Particular suggestions and ideas about materials included:
- *Wellington Square, Fuzzbuzz, Oxford Reading Tree* materials.
- *PAT* (Phonological Awareness Training).
- *Jolly Phonics.*
- Rhyme and analogy work.
- Tactile resources such as alphabet mats.
- Silly sentence dominoes.
- *The Hickey Multi-sensory Language Course.*
- *Listen and Do, What's Different, Things that go together, Starter Stile,* fine motor skills activities etc.

To conclude, the pupils' self-esteem is crucial to success.

Concluding remarks

Primary school teachers are realistic about how well they feel the Hour has been working with their particular pupils. Rather than saying that they have sent in negative comments it could be said that those which show reservations are based in practice and have not been expressed lightly. They state what could be changed within the organisation of the Hour and how they feel that special educational needs was a 'bolt-on' rather than an integral part of the Framework. One SENCO felt that Framework is too prescriptive and teachers' professional judgements cannot be used. It was noted by the SENCO of one of the middle schools that if there are additional adults, children with special educational needs can benefit from remaining within the 'main' group, but if there are no such supporters, these pupils either end up doing 'holding activities' or they become disruptive.

An infants school staff wrote quite fully as they felt that hearing children reading individually has suffered because of lack of time and also that there have been fewer opportunities for children to change their books and for the teachers to make notes to parents. Also they found that some children with learning difficulties could sit passively during the whole class teaching for long periods and that they did not have access to speedy reinforcement during the 20-minute group work. Children with specific learning difficulties made very slow progress as they found it hard to keep up with the pace of introducing new sounds and concepts and that the demands made on them were too rapid. However, the staff found that some pupils had made very pleasing progress and that word level work had supported reading development although not necessarily comprehension.

Other comments included:
- The whole class text work was found to be enjoyable for all pupils but overall the *National Literacy Strategy* as a Programme of Study is pitched at an incorrect level for children with special educational needs and is not flexible enough. (Village school)
- With infants with special educational needs even the simplified texts can be too difficult for sight word retention. Other ideas such as flashcards are necessary. (Infants school)
- Where pupils fail to make progress it is felt that the *National Literacy Strategy* does not cater for individual pupils with special needs. Extra support is needed so that these children can work at their own pace and build on skills with confidence. (Primary school)
- There has been no time to deliver appropriate individual programmes. An increase in constant low level disruption and an increase in break and lunch time poor behaviour has been noted. Less able children are becoming less able. (Primary school in a 'deprived' area)
- Concern has been felt over lack of opportunities for extended writing. There has been insufficient time for careful planning, discussion and completion of work by pupils. (Primary school)

- It has been found that withdrawal group children made good progress if they are at Code of Practice Stages 1 and 2 but those on Stage 3 made little or no progress. There were slight improvements in reading but concerns are expressed about writing as children with learning problems often haven't finished work, resulting in numerous pieces of incomplete stories etc. (Junior school)
- It was felt that some children with special educational needs did benefit from raised expectations but individual reading was still needed for these children as guided reading is not enough. The very weak child who can only read a few words and who cannot be accommodated in any guided reading group needs specialised help. (Infants school)
- The staff are in favour of the Literacy Strategy Framework for all pupils except those who have special educational needs on the Code of Practice Stages 2 and above. It is difficult to incorporate pupils with particular special educational needs into the class in an appropriate and effective way. (Primary school)

Positive comments which conclude this chapter on an optimistic note are:
- A particular plus is that many aspects of language such as the teaching of phonics and grammar, traditionally the province of the special needs teacher, are now part of mainstream teaching. (Large primary school)
- It has given children with special educational needs independent tasks that they can do but which also further their development. (Primary school)
- The SENCO had started to use some of the ALS materials since the beginning of July which had been modified to work with larger groups. This has benefited all the Year 4 pupils. (Primary school)
- The Literacy Hour is good and enjoyed by children. (Primary school)
- There must be a balance between keeping the children focused, involved and interested whilst not holding others back in the shared part of the Hour. (Church of England primary school)
- The staff have 'really enjoyed the challenge' as they feel that the organisation within the school is well set up and that pupils' standards have risen. Also the pupils' expectations have been raised. The ASC teacher-in-charge has found that much of her time has been spent on redesigning worksheets and searching for appropriate books but as the ASC children really enjoy their lessons 'it has been worthwhile'. (Middle school)
- For pupils with specific learning difficulties the whole class teaching is often supportive in methods and in repetition of vocabulary and terms. Phonic focus is also beneficial. Pupils with sensory and physical needs have participated well with appropriate resources and support. (Suburban school)
- Children have enjoyed being part of a group and doing literacy when everybody else is. Children enjoyed the session being broken up into the four parts as moving from task to task helped their concentration. (Large junior school)
- Children are benefiting greatly. (Primary school)
- On the whole the *National Literacy Strategy* has been met with appreciation of its relevance as a guide to progression. (Primary school 300+)

It is hoped that, after the Literacy Hour has been in operation for more time, any problems experienced will have been settled and that appropriate resources in terms of finances and adult support have been provided.

NASEN Northants: Branch Response

E. Bentley, J. Harris and I. Robinson

The Northants Branch of NASEN collated the views from several schools within the county. These included mainstream and special schools, Key Stages 1 and 2. Literacy co-ordinators, SENCOs and class teachers contributed to the collective response.

Description of Literacy Hour arrangements and how pupils with special educational needs accessed the Hour

The special school's arrangements are setting throughout the school. In mainstream the arrangements vary in Key Stages 1 and 2 as there is some withdrawal for group work and some setting, in some of the schools from Year 2 onwards. Groups are often 'set' by literacy ability and in some schools pupils with special educational needs are withdrawn for the complete Hour. Views varied about the problems presented by pupils with special educational needs. In some schools it is felt that shared text is often above the receptive language of certain pupils and even with differentiated questioning a few pupils are 'lost'. However, pupils with dyslexic problems are given the opportunity to shine and demonstrate their verbal abilities. Generally the sharing of the story works well but pupils with special educational needs often have difficulties in coping with the more specific aspects of grammar etc. A variety of approaches were used such as streaming, withdrawal and additional teaching support. The latter is particularly used when pupils have behavioural difficulties. It was noted that skilled staff are required to handle specific special educational needs and that help with differentiation is needed from the SENCO in order to help other members of staff to cater for small special needs groups.

Resource implications

This survey noted the following:

- In order to use parental support effectively in school INSET is needed.
- There is the need for additional adults to help vary tasks and to break these up into smaller, more manageable units.
- Where untrained staff are used there is the need for training (and it was noted that often such staff members are not paid whilst undertaking training).
- A wide variety of materials are needed in order for the Hour to run successfully.
- Because Learning Support Assistants are required to support the Literacy Hour there should be a pay structure which recognises their work and experience and encourages their training.

Other pointers

The sub-committee collating the responses are in agreement that the *National Literacy Strategy* is a positive Strategy and that it will raise standards if resourced effectively. Responses stated:

- The general class teacher is actually teaching specific skills which in the past were often incidental. Thus it is felt that the results are already positive.
- However, it is noted that a correct pace for the Hour is vital as the time factor is important for some pupils.
- Some pupils with special educational needs are not able to work independently for the length of time expected of them.
- The Literacy Strategy has posed a threat for some adults because it has raised expectation and, therefore, it has made some staff feel insecure.

The Literacy Hour from the Viewpoint of an SEN Support Teacher

Anne Dutton

My role and my school

I work as a support teacher, in a large primary school, with seven children with Statements for Special Educational Needs. All have general learning difficulties and some have other difficulties related to speech, hearing and behaviour. Their attainment in English is between Level 1 and Level 3. Each child's Statement allocates them 3.25 hours of teacher support time a week and two also have ancillary support. I am in school for a large part of the week and as I often work with the children in groups I have a considerable amount of contact time with each of them.

When our school became a pilot school for the Literacy Hour it was necessary to consider carefully with our SENCO and Literacy Co-ordinator just what my role was to be. We were aware that these children were required to be in with their peers and we wanted to use the time to its best advantage. We tried various strategies and developed our plan of working for this year from what we learnt.

Organising my work

The school has three mixed-ability Year 5 and 6 classes and there are two or three of 'my children' in each class. The team of teachers meet together to plan for the Literacy Hour.

We decided that I would join one class on a Monday, the second on a Tuesday and the third on a Wednesday and support the children within the lesson. I was doubtful at first that there would be much value in me being in the room for the teacher-led part of the Hour but my doubts were soon dispelled.

The children's attention wanders quickly but they can be brought back on task with a quick nod or gesture. When they can check that their response to a question is acceptable they are more confident to join in with the class. They often query things that they have not understood at a later time. They are more secure in their approach to individual work because of the support they receive within the class lesson once a week.

Independent work is set by the class teacher with regard to the child's IEP. This links in with that set for the rest of the ability group but may be differentiated. On other occasions I lead guided text work, as planned with the class teacher, for the group. The advantage of this is that the children are not seen to be receiving special attention but are working successfully within the class.

I do not stay in for the plenary session but read with one of the children.

Thursday is a different day. This time I am in charge of the seven with an ancillary to support me! This time more emphasis is given to:

- phonic skills and phonological awareness
- high frequency words
- sentence building.

Over the year the children have modelled their behaviour and responses on those that they have observed in the other children. They are now more likely to respond in complete sentences, use a wider vocabulary, understand how to look at text for meaning and are more confident in their ability to work independently.

On Fridays all three classes spend time on extended writing. Again I work with the group and an ancillary. We spend the first part of the Hour on shared writing and then consider how the children will plan their own writing. They do not find ordering ideas easy, and story boards and their own drawing have recently helped to overcome some of the difficulties. We try to give them as many strategies for spelling as possible. They now enjoy reading their work to each other and on occasions recording it onto a tape recorder. They are all making progress and enjoy celebrating their success.

I feel we have been able to use the Framework of the Literacy Hour for the benefit of these children and that the doubts I had about them being bored, lost or floundering were largely unfounded.

Teaching the Literacy Strategy: A Class Teacher's Perspective

Pauline M. Smith

I have been teaching for nearly 30 years and have seen many changes to the curriculum and the ways of working with children. One thing I have learnt is to be adaptable as there is always another change just around the corner.

Personalising the Literacy Strategy

When the Literacy Project began I looked carefully at it. I could see it had a lot of good points but also there were going to be problems. My school has now been undertaking work from the Literacy Strategy for nearly two years so I have had more time to practise and experiment than many other teachers.

The most important thing I found is that the Literacy Strategy must not be considered as written in stone and therefore unchangeable. The nature of each class will make that impossible. Therefore the most important thing I learnt was that if it did not work then adapt it. As long as the criteria were being met in a similar way then go with it.

My first hurdle was that I teach in a mixed year group (Years 3 and 4) and the Literacy Strategy does not really cater for this. (Thank goodness this problem seems to have been tackled in the Numeracy Project.) I am the school SEN co-ordinator and this year I had more than half the class on the Special Needs Register. Most had general learning difficulties but some had more specific problems. So what was I to do? Good organisation of the session along with the planning was going to be vital as well as providing the best resources especially for the independent groups.

Organising groups and time

I had found that working with four groups suited me the best (even though I had a class of 36) as this gave me one day a week where I was not working with a specific group and could, therefore, work with individuals, as necessary. I split each year group into two using general reading ability as the simple criterion. These groups generally stayed the same but sometimes I would change then depending on what it was I wanted to teach. I found that the way the Literacy Hour is organised does not lend itself to extended periods of writing. I tried working the Literacy Hour for four days and using the fifth day for writing but this did not really work as I found it difficult to work with individuals. I discovered that taking a whole week and concentrating on writing in each session worked a lot better as I could work with groups or individuals when necessary.

I worked on a four-week cycle. Weeks 1, 2 and 3 were for Guided Reading whilst Week 4 was an Extended Writing week. I also set aside one extra lesson each week where the children could use books for research, reviews, making compilations etc. so that I could then hear children read independently or in small groups. This meant that the children who needed extra time for reading could be given it without missing out on other lessons or subjects.

Each week I planned four independent activities although I did sometimes have a learning support assistant working with me and this was taken into account when planning. One activity would be a follow-up to the Guided Reading or Writing session that the children had done the day or week before. One activity would be specifically aimed at work on spelling. The remaining two activities would vary depending on what was being taught that week (eg comprehension, word searching, cloze texts, computer work etc.). The day I had a free session could come at any time of the week depending on which group I wanted to work with. I did not always work with the lower ability groups but tried to spread my time as evenly as possible.

Working with a wide range of abilities

Working in the two class sessions at the beginning of the lesson could have been a problem with such a wide range of abilities. However, this did not happen as I tried to find ways that would involve the whole class all the time. Sometimes the questioning was specific to one of the groups or general to the whole class. However, this seemed to exclude the insecure and the lazy. I had to find ways of involving all the children and in such a way that they did not fear failure. One way I solved this was to give each child a set of cards with the alphabet on them and another set with the vowel sounds (double vowels for instance) that were being looked at that week. When asked to spell a word the children could make them with their cards and then show them. All the children became involved and cheered when they got the answer correct. The ones who were incorrect did not feel embarrassed as no one else saw their answers except me. This is just one example of activities that can be provided in order to involve the whole class. Children were encouraged to discuss answers in pairs, then in fours and then back to the class.

Covering the stages

For the group work I always plan on the continuum. That is I start with the easiest concept and work through the stages to the hardest. I looked at the term plans for my two year groups and found the areas that complemented each other. One example of this is Years 3 and 4 term 1. Year 3 children should work on verbs while the Year 4 children extended their knowledge of verbs and then went on to adverbs. I would introduce the subject for all at the lower level with a mention of the higher level and as each group was ready to move on I would give them input during my free session each week. The beauty of this way of working is that once the work is planned to cover all the stages it is planned for whatever class one has within that age group. The work I planned last year I am using again this year. The children who were Year 3 last year will not do the same work again as they will have moved onto the next stage.

As I mentioned at the beginning, change is always just around the corner. My children have been targeted for the Additional Literacy Support this year and this will bring new problems. I am not sure yet if my framework will work within such a regimented system but only time will tell. And that will be another story.

George Learns to Read

Tessa Knott

Once upon a time, in a classroom not too far away, a small boy crept out from under the table (where he had been snacking on his friend's leg) and feeling the force of the Literacy Hour, he learnt to read... (with apologies to 'Star Wars').

The story continues

Getting into trouble was definitely one of the things George did best. It was his most effective strategy for avoiding all the things he found difficult. This included just about everything he was required to do in school: reading, writing, maths, making friends. No wonder he couldn't cope with 20 minutes independent working when his teacher's attention was focused elsewhere.

Miraculously, after six months, George came up to me and said, 'Miss, I can read now, can't I?' What had happened? Had the Literacy Strategy really come up with ideas no one had yet thought of?

Of course, the reality of the situation is not quite as simple. The Literacy Strategy was one element amongst many that may have helped or hindered George's progress. First and foremost, for whatever reason, George decided to do some work. Not a lot, but it was a start. When he started to do some work he discovered he was really rather good at some things - he could beat anyone in the class at mental maths. He grasped new concepts quickly, could explain his work; his confidence and self-esteem soared.

The role of the Literacy Strategy for George

So what role did the Literacy Strategy have in George learning to read?

First of all, I firmly believe that George would have received high-quality teaching in reading and writing regardless of the introduction of the Literacy Hour. Furthermore the Additional Guidance acknowledges that some children with special educational needs will require additional time outside the Hour to work on their objectives.

This was certainly true for George. No one in George's family reads fluently, so it has always been essential for George to read daily to his class teacher. It is not practical to build this into the structure of the Literacy Hour and continued outside it, as it would have done anyway. I believe this to be one of the major factors contributing to George learning to read.

However, shared reading within the Hour provided George with access to a far wider variety of texts than he could access himself, even with support. This was aided in part by some of the excellent materials produced by some publishers in response to the Literacy Strategy. He could not maintain concentration to follow a shared text from a Big Book or OHP, but if, after an initial reading with the class, the teacher then 'shared' his own copy of the text while making whole class teaching points, George could be kept on task. As we have seen, George shines in oral work and the introduction and plenary sessions allowed him plenty of opportunity to contribute.

Independence and the Literacy Hour

Independent written work remained a nightmare for George (and his teacher!). The only way to keep him on task was to provide work that was so well within his capability it provided very little learning experience, and to check on him every five minutes or so.

George is certainly not alone in needing regular attention and reassurance. Many children with special educational needs find it difficult to follow more than one or two instructions at a time, even when tasks are appropriately differentiated. Consequently the class teacher needs to check regularly to ensure the child stays on task and knows what to do next.

This makes it extremely difficult to implement the focused 20 minutes guided group work. In a class with a high percentage of children with special educational needs, the teacher needs to work with the group, set them a small task such as discuss the main subject of a paragraph, whizz round the class checking on the Georges and return to discover their findings.

George certainly benefited from the high expectation and use of praise specifically identified in the Strategy. But I would hope those features were there in any lesson!

The benefits of the Literacy Strategy

However, where I think the Literacy Strategy has really benefited not just the George or the average Georgina Bloggs at Anytown Primary, is that it has opened up lively debate about the quality of teaching and learning that goes on in our classrooms. Ideas are being discussed and argued about in staffrooms. In our school we have been observing each other's lessons, resulting in a lot of shared ideas. Anything that turns more teachers into thinking practitioners has to be a good thing!

Government directives will come and go. We will still be there in the classroom with George.

So how is he getting on now? The short answer is I don't know. As so often seems to happen, just as you think you are making a breakthrough, the family upped sticks and disappeared. So, if you meet a young man with a taste for human legs and work evasion tactics that the Artful Dodger would be proud of, encourage him to read. It could be George!

Twenty Ways to Make the Hour Work

Adapted from suggestions from Linda Care

- Trust your own professional judgement. If existing systems are working for your pupils evaluate them and integrate them.
- Often children do not like too much change. Therefore, a carousel of different activities going on within one classroom is not necessarily helpful. Differentiate activities from the same task for different ability levels.
- Be flexible. Be prepared to group children for reasons other than that of ability. Grouping for social reasons can create a better working environment.
- Be flexible with the material. There needs to be a balance of word/sentence/text over the week. Pace your lessons but don't stop pupils and change to something else if they are keen to carry on and finish.
- Trust your own judgement as to how the pupils' learning needs can best be met by the management of groups within the classroom. Some pupils might not be able to cope with a whole group session for 20 minutes so would need to be moved away to focus for ten minutes on a specific related activity.
- Demonstrate grammatical points into the whole group session by modelling correct language structure rather than giving more 'formal' teaching.
- Devise or use an existing rewards system for any particular area you wish to target, eg working faster or more independently.
- Focus attention and speed up independent working by playing a piece of music or using a timer (eg how many words beginning with 'st' can you find in the text before the music stops?).
- Remember that multi-sensory approaches can be very successful (eg clapping syllables, hearing and saying sounds, singing, using colour, working with magnetic and sandpaper letters etc.).
- Keep parents informed. There are booklets published for parents or schools could devise their own.
- Use as many lists of books as you can find to inform your choice of books.
- Simplify your planning as far as this is possible. Don't feel that you have to reinvent the wheel but be prepared to look at what publishers and advisers etc. from your LEA have done for you.
- Some publishers have published structured courses which can be very useful. Use and adapt these.
- Spend some money on buying the correct sized book stand as this will make life easier. Folding wire book stands for Big Books can be purchased as well as freestanding magnetic whiteboards complete with book stands.
- Use large acetate sheets clipped over the pages of Big Books so that pupils can write and highlight points directly over the text.
- Consider using individual magnetic whiteboards for pupils to practise writing and using magnetic letters.
- Use story audio tapes with headphones as independent tasks.
- Teach punctuation in the whole group reading session by giving pupils punctuation picture cards or polystyrene shapes to hold up whenever they see the punctuation as the text is read. Sounds for punctuation could be used but this could become rather noisy!
- Make learning practical. Make things with the pupils such as letter wheels, rolls for onset and rime, simple board games to review main points of a longer story. If learning is fun the children will remember.

- Celebrate reading by having a special assembly or evening when teachers and parents as well as pupils read their favourite short stories (or parts of stories) and poems. Have high profile awards such as readership certificates and book trail awards. Make sure that children with special educational needs are able to gain these. Raise the profile of reading in school. Make a visual impact such as growing a reading tree in the entrance hall. Start with a bare tree shape and encourage pupils to write the name of a book that they have read and enjoyed onto a leaf shape and add this to the tree.

The Literacy Hour at Bell Lane Primary School

Susy Stone

Bell Lane is a large multicultural primary in London of just under 320 pupils with 93 children on the SEN Register. It is vertically grouped from Year 1 with three classes in each year group. Pupil turnover is very high. It was designated a 'target school' and at the end of the summer of 1999 the school showed a 17% improvement in Key Stage 2 SATs results. Pupils on Stage 2 of the Code of Practice made great strides with their literacy acquisition. However, there was some concern about pupils on Stage 3.

The school organises the *National Literacy Strategy* through whole class teaching with setting for additional spelling sessions. Pupils on Stage 3 of the Code of Practice have parallel withdrawal Literacy Hour sessions for one-fifth of the week. The SENCO is the Deputy Head and she teaches 3.5 days of support per week. A second support teacher teaches two days per week. There is also a Stage 3 teacher who works with 11 pupils for one morning per week. Two Learning Support Assistants are employed and part of their role includes in-class support.

In November 1998 the Regional Director of the *National Literacy Strategy* visited the school and the following presentation was made.

Strengths
- Detailed focus on text;
- Big Books are a very good resource, particularly poetry and information texts;
- structured grammar teaching;
- guided reading and writing are good activities, though not necessarily every day;
- children enjoy sharing work in plenary;
- children are doing literacy work at home of their own accord (eg poetry);
- Reception classes are doing well with group reading;
- support teachers have a clearer focus for their work;
- IEPs are easier to write;
- there is more diversity of content than previously;
- the introductory session is successful;
- children up to Year 4 like the carpet and the Big Books;
- repetition is good and 'produces the goods' (eg whole class knowing what a non-fiction text is);
- punctuation is being covered well.

Concerns
- The appropriateness of teaching 4 and 5 year-olds in the same way as 10 and 11 year-olds;
- older pupils resent being made to sit on the carpet and they consider Big Books babyish;
- the appropriateness of teaching literacy in the same format every day;
- the Literacy Hour does not prepare older pupils for secondary school English teaching;
- time constraints 'stop the flow' of creative and poetry writing;
- other adults supporting pupils during the introduction can be a distraction;
- mistakes in independent group tasks can become entrenched before the teacher has a chance to pick them up;
- single phonic focus for the week with such a wide range of needs;
- top level spellers are not 'stretched';
- traditional 'story time' is a victim of time constraints and of statutory time on carpet;
- Key Stage 1 teachers are unsure of their role in a 10-minute guided session;
- carpet session is too long for pupils with poor concentration;

- corrections are often not done, done out of context or not done alongside the child;
- teacher as scribe - staff feel they are not providing a good model of presentation and have to stop pupils' 'flow' to write a sentence;
- there are not enough Big Books, as these are costly and they quickly become 'tatty'.

There is particular concern that the school is losing ground where the teaching of spelling is concerned. In 1993, significant work in this area was undertaken, led by the school's two specialist language support teachers, with considerable additional expert input. This informed the teaching of spelling in the school and the results improved but the constraints of the *National Literacy Strategy* seem to be preventing the previous direct focus on the teaching of spelling. Similar concerns are felt about handwriting as staff feel they are not able to give the specific individual attention to handwriting as they did previously.

It had been suggested that time be taken from science to allow for additional literacy. Science was another area of the curriculum which had improved because of focused input from co-ordinators released to work alongside teachers. This had particular implications for pupils, many of whom do not have English as a first language, who found it hard to clearly explain what they understand. The staff were unhappy about the prospect of compromising their progress in science and, therefore, are grappling with finding extra literacy time while still providing a broad and balanced curriculum.

Some problems already overcome
- Planning has become much quicker;
- concerns about the pace of work in independent group tasks have lessened;
- Years 5/6 have overcome the Big Books resource issue by planning on a three-week cycle;
- funds that the PTA gave helped to resource the *National Literacy Strategy;*
- commission from a Scholastic book fair has helped to solve a resource issue concerning thesauruses;
- extra literacy time has been found for extended writing;
- ways of working with EAL and SEN support staff have been refined.

Points from the Regional Director's feedback
- Although the initial National Literacy Project was very directive the aim is that now schools should have ownership of the Framework and use it in accordance with their own circumstances;
- laminating the tops of Big Books might extend their life span;
- the *National Literacy Strategy* is being extended into the secondary sector, initially with Year 7 teachers, with the focus being literacy across the curriculum (Bell Lane staff suggested that Years 6 and 7 members of staff plan together);
- flexibility was stressed so that items can transfer from one day to the next. He felt that the school was providing variety in approaches;
- the introductory session should be interactive and a range of activities should avoid this seeming too long;
- children do not have to sit on the carpet and Big Books do not always have to be used;
- the Hour can be used as time to prepare pupils for a literacy task to do as an extended activity;
- he advocated marking as a group activity;
- he suggested that word level work is pitched 'as high as you dare';
- time must be made for the loss of story time;
- any concerns that staff have about their role in guided sessions should be addressed by training;
- OHPs can be used for modelling handwriting;
- teachers of EAL pupils should be able to give more specific input for their particular pupils.

Key Stage 1	Key Stage 2
• Weekly planning meeting. SENCO contributes ideas and resources.	• Weekly planning meeting. SENCO contributes ideas and resources.
• Planning currently follows Year 1 scheme NLS (2-year cycle).	• Planning currently follows Year 3 and Year 5 scheme NLS (2-year cycle).
• Learning Support Assistant as other adult one day a week in each class.	• Learning Support Assistant as other adult one day a week in each class.
• One day a week SENCO alternates between two of the classes, does word level introduction and works as other adult with focus group including Stage 2 pupils.	• Stage 2 support - 3 withdrawal groups across year group. - 30 mins per week tracking back word level work in NLS. Some use of ICT with software targeted at SEN pupils; - speaking and listening 1 hour per week, based on class text level focus, and supporting grammar and punctuation objectives of NLS; - writing 1 hour per week based on text/word/sentence level objectives of NLS, including tracking back.
• Stage 2 Support: 2 withdrawal support groups across year group, comprising Year 2 pupils, which initially focused on word level work. (The focus can change to sentence level work).	
• Group of mostly Year 1 pupils identified who are not keeping pace with word level work. These need some extra support.	• Stage 3 support teacher takes one Year 3/4 group and one Year 5/6 group. In 3/4 she is in class for the whole session. In 5/6 she does parallel introduction and group work and returns for the plenary.
• Trialling group IEPs for Stage 2 based on NLS objectives. Model written by SENCO but will be written by year group teachers. Stage 3 pupils have individual IEPs with literacy targets based on the NLS.	• IEPs as for Key Stage 1.
• Additional literacy. - setted spelling group 30 mins per week - 4 sets with SENCO taking the lowest ability. Friday pm introduction to word level work for the following week; - handwriting as part of a 'carousel' afternoon; - each class has an ICT literacy session 1 hour per week.	• Additional Literacy. - extended writing 30 mins per week added to 1 Literacy Hour; - Year 5/6 spelling 30 mins per week in 4 setted groups, SENCO taking lowest ability.

SEN organisation and the Literacy Hour.

Secondary Schools and the Hour: 'Adapting the Hour'

Dorothy Smith

Six secondary schools responded to the pro forma from England, Scotland and Wales. Five were comprehensive schools (one of which was grant maintained) and the other was a High School technology college. Only one school had less than 1000 pupils, in fact one was very large with 1400 eleven to eighteen year-olds.

Pupils with special educational needs and their particular problems in coping with the Hour

All the schools had a high percentage of pupils with special educational needs. One of the comprehensive schools had 200 pupils on its SEN register, about 15% of the pupil population, and out of this number there were 38 pupils with a Statement (25 with moderate learning difficulties and 13 with specific learning difficulties). This school mentioned that because of special schools closing there were more pupils with moderate learning difficulties entering and that its Year 7 contained about 80 pupils on the Special Needs Register, about half the intake. Another of the comprehensive schools stressed that its pupil support base was split into two sets. One of these contained those pupils with learning difficulties (which includes a full spectrum of learning need) and the other with pupils with emotional and behavioural problems but, as the writer explained, there is overlap between the clientele. This school runs an inclusion strategy especially as there is no special school within local boundaries. Another of the comprehensive schools ran two schools within one as the school was divided into two bands. A Literacy Hour-style teaching approach was being piloted with four groups of 97 pupils with two groups of the ten least able and another two groups of around 15 who were working around Levels 3-4. This school had already found that the present Year 7 intake were noticeably more positive and well-motivated and that the headteachers of the feeder primary schools were reporting that the Literacy Hour was making pupils more motivated and helping to build their confidence.

The reading and spelling problems differed in the schools ranging from actual non-readers and writers or those with literacy attainment scores of around 6 to 7 years to pupils helped with reading up to reading ages of 10½ years. This comprehensive school focused upon reading skills and the pupils' ability to transfer these into other areas of the curriculum. It organised small groups of one to four or one to six with the aim to raise reading ages to 11 years by the end of Year 7 and to 12 years by the end of Key Stage 3. Older pupils were noted as having low self-esteem and confidence and it was difficult to convince them that they were not unintelligent. If they hadn't made progress by Year 9 lack of motivation was seen and their teachers had to find alternative methods in order to revisit and reinforce teaching points. The smaller school felt that there were no problems which could be termed out of the ordinary and the school made sure that unfinished written tasks were not seen as a failure and the pupils were congratulated on what they had achieved rather than being shown what they hadn't completed.

Literacy Hour arrangements

One of the larger comprehensive schools had two teaching staff and eight part-time learning support assistants (LSAs) in the special needs department. The SENCO was on the Senior Management Team but did not undertake specialist special needs teaching or administration. This school organised a very successful summer school in August 1999 which was felt to form a strong basis for literacy teaching within the school. Another high school explained that there was LSA allocation to the groups containing the least able pupils. The other schools had differing types of literacy organisation and not all could be termed an 'Hour'. There were setted classes, whole class work, extended reading sessions, concentrated periods of reading in literacy lessons, the establishment of a successful literacy week, withdrawal sessions, 'reading booster groups', whole school screening of reading levels and extraction of those pupils requiring help. One school set up an intervention strategy based on Literacy Hour format with Year 7 but unlike the primary sector this was one hour per week structured literacy instruction.

Strategies to overcome problems

Each school mentioned ways that were felt to be helpful in their own situations. Some overlapped or were duplicated and the following list shows the variety of ideas, methods and systems which might add to readers' current practices.

- Mixture of extraction from mainstream subjects and in-class support.
- Curriculum adaptations and differentiation.
- Special arrangements for tests and exams (the use of readers and/or scribes).
- ICT (Correction and SuccessMaker).
- Employment of special educational needs learning support assistants.
- Many literacy programmes particularly SRA.
- Time spent on Reading Recovery so that all pupils could read even at a basic level.
- Praise and congratulation.
- Clear 'goals' - short achievable targets set. Revisiting and overlearning.
- Short tasks with several changes of activity in each hour lesson.
- Reward systems - verbal praise, 'stickers' on work, merits, certificates.
- Involving parents (Paired Reading, Home/school reading programmes).
- Whole school policy supported by Head and Senior Management Team with a cross-curricular group who meet regularly.
- English Policy which focuses upon raising literacy.
- SEN faculty who co-ordinate extraction and screen the whole school (an additional adult employed specifically to teach reading groups).
- Primary/secondary cross-phase group.
- Staff INSET training.
- Simple and achievable target setting and a reward system which was given for effort in meeting these targets.

Resource implications

There were many factors mentioned in this category. Some were suggestions for organisation, others were positive outcomes whilst some outlined the difficulties.

Ideas for further organisation
- Reduction of the curriculum for those with specific learning difficulties to work on remaining subjects which leads to many excellent exam results.
- More staffing (teachers and LSAs) required to support pupils in mainstream classes effectively.
- Resources funded through generous capitation.
- Summer school good because of the small groups (8/9 with teacher/LSA/sixth form help) and improvements in test scores seen after two weeks plus incredible increase in self-esteem.

Positive outcomes
- SRA Reading Programme effective for many pupils.
- Multi-sensory programmes work.
- Computer programmes work.
- Spellcheckers work.

- Shared reading and DARTS (working together in groups) work.
- Individual attention helps to meet individual targets.
- If the theme is correct this is helpful.
- A variety of activity and pace.
- Writing frames used as a base for written work.
- Spelling rules learnt and tested daily.
- Daily reading activities are important.

Difficulties
- Lists of spellings (unrelated to texts used) do not work.
- Too many worksheets do not work.
- Not enough time for complex lesson planning or working out schemes of work so 'off the shelf' materials are needed.
- Arrangements do not 'pick up' those pupils with specific learning difficulties so these will need a similar approach but at a different time.

Concluding remarks

The idea of a Literacy Hour is too new for schools in the secondary sector to have come to grips with different organisational structures and alternative ways of working. Therefore, the points that the respondents made were sometimes positive, sometimes questioning of what was expected of them and sometimes they were statements of concern.

One school felt that its wide range of special educational needs were difficult to manage in a large mainstream school and, although inclusion was thought to be desirable, it was felt that any inclusion policy needs to be proactive rather than being rather inflexible and forced on the school. However, as another school stated, any chance to spend time with pupils and to improve literacy levels is to be welcomed and one school which hasn't used the Key Stage 3 Literacy Hour arrangements has adapted ideas and the format. The shared reading and the work generated from this have been most successful with pupils with special educational needs in Key Stage 3. A note of caution was made in one response that within the secondary phase the Literacy Hour is fine for the average and above average pupils but probably not so good for pupils with special educational needs, especially those with moderate and specific learning difficulties. These pupils are not able to achieve well as the texts are geared to the more able reader. They need a version of the Literacy Hour which works at a slower pace using more suitable books. Spelling has to be structured and taught by multi-sensory methods. Special needs pupils find everything goes too quickly and thus they fall by the wayside.

As the Literacy Hour becomes established in the primary sector it will be interesting to see how the reading and spelling attainments of Year 6 pupils increase making the work of the secondary sector easier, it is to be hoped. One school felt that primary schools were not sufficiently well resourced, especially in terms of extra adult support, in order to address the issue of early identification. This school's respondent concluded by hoping that the Government's plan for 15,000 extra learning support assistants will help (especially in rural primary schools attempting to deliver to three year groups in one class). Then there may only be the entrenched literacy problems for the secondary schools to work with rather than many of the present underperforming pupils. It was most pleasing that there were returns from secondary schools because it shows that, even though there might be concerns, these schools are giving thought to how they can support literacy teaching. It is an interesting point that most of the returns did not state that improving reading and spelling skills should be a whole school issue, one that is worked on by the English department and supported by other curriculum areas, and not just the work of the special needs or learning support departments.

John Bentley 'Beachcombers': Summer Literacy School 1999
(Article written for the school magazine)

Patricia Wilde

John Bentley School was buzzing with activity for two weeks of the summer holiday when the 'Beachcombers' took over the Support department and other areas of the school, and worked hard on their literacy skills, while having great fun doing so.

Funded by the Government, in their initiative to raise standards of literacy amongst 11 year-olds, the Beachcombers were carefully selected by their primary schools as being students who needed an extra boost to their reading and writing skills in order to approach secondary school with renewed confidence and expertise.

As co-ordinator of the scheme, I am elated by the success of this venture and hope that it will continue for the next two years. The benefits to the students have been enormous and each one has improved their scores on standardised reading and spelling tests, as well as visibly growing in maturity and confidence as the days went by.

Emphasising writing skills

The Summer School curriculum was carefully structured using the Literacy Hour format for academic work, based on the overall theme of the Sea. The teaching team decided to put emphasis on writing skills, as many of our students had reasonable reading skills, but found it difficult to express themselves in written form.

The 35 students were divided into groups of eight to nine and to foster the club atmosphere were given tutor names: Sharks, Crabs, Clowns and Pirates. Each group had a tutor (two secondary, two primary) and an assistant working with them, as well as numerous volunteer helpers from the sixth form and my Year 10 tutor group. As a consequence it was possible to give each student individual help in attempting to reach the literacy targets they had to set themselves for the ten days of the Summer School.

At 8.30 each morning the students started on their word level work with their tutors for the first half hour; ie spelling, grammar, games, worksheets and shared texts. At 9 a.m. they moved on to another tutor in another room, on a carousel, to explore a different genre of writing; narrative, report and recount, explanatory and persuasive. This gave the students the experience of different styles of teaching and room changes that they would experience at John Bentley.

The final aim was to produce a 'best book' for each tutor group, in which they would display what they had learnt during their ten-day intensive literacy training. This excellent work is displayed in school at the moment, and you can see some good examples of the four genres, which is well presented and of a high standard in quality. The teaching team consider that these students strived to reach the Level 4 which had eluded some of them in the SATs, and in most cases succeeded.

Reading as well

Reading was not neglected, as the students studied a group reader as well as taking home individual readers each day, to read with parents and record in a reading log. Homework played a big part in the literacy improvements made, as spelling, reading and writing exercises were set each day and marked each morning. Most of the students did this diligently and gained stamps for their labours which were later exchanged for prizes. Homework was established early on, as part of the requirements of secondary school life.

Practical afternoons

The intensive four-hour morning session was balanced equally with practical activities, which normally took place in the afternoons, after a delicious lunch and time to let off steam outside, weather permitting. In addition we had visitors to the school who inspired and entertained us. Mike Leigh, an Australian poet, showed us his slides of the Australian outback and wildlife, read us his own poetry, and challenged us to write our own poetry about England for a competition. Our students rose to the challenge and produced some excellent poetry, which Mike came back to judge and present prizes of poetry books. During the second week, Mike Smith and Nicky came to read and dramatise Mike's children's book, *Castle Freke*, and challenged our students to write a suitable Chapter 5. There were some superb attempts and some of our most timid students found the courage to read their work aloud to the group.

The highlight of the fortnight was the trip to Weston-Super-Mare and, despite previous appalling weather, the sun shone for us on that day. We visited the Sea Life Centre, where we were able to handle starfish and small crabs and stroke the ray; as well as don 3-D glasses to solve the sea life quiz. Lunch on the beach was followed by an energetic game of soccer and a more sedate game of rounders. This was followed by a visit to Hutton Moor swimming pool. Ice-creams were devoured by all, and postcards written to parents and posted, before we all climbed back onto the coach to arrive back at school after 6 p.m. It was a long day, but great fun.

It amazed me to discover just how much the students had learned and retained about sea creatures; through the visit, the books read and the reports written. When they were asked 50 questions in the Sea Life quiz during the second week the Clowns got them all right, including the spelling of crustacean.

The students' energy and enthusiasm for the topic never flagged and during the second week they brought in articles about the sighting of a Great White Shark off the coast of Cornwall, which they had found themselves. In addition we are now great defenders of all sharks and whales and will only eat tuna if it has a dolphin on the tin, denoting that they have been caught in dolphin free nets!

Mr Gunston worked hard to help us to create a storm using a motley assortment of percussion instruments, including old saucepans and pop bottles. This was made into a sound poem, using storm adjectives, and performed for the parents on the last afternoon. As can be imagined this was a very popular activity! Mr Rahman also joined us for some fun activities, which included 'who wants to be a Muffinaire?' based on the well-known TV programme, and using spelling questions and general knowledge, as well as his usual mental arithmetic problems. All the students loved this.

On the last Friday afternoon, about 60 parents joined us in the Drama Studio for the Celebration ceremony, where the students' work was displayed for the parents to see. Mrs Burrell and the Lady Mayor, Mrs Smith, helped us to celebrate our success and the students performed a few poems and songs. The sound poem had its first public performance and then all the students were presented with their certificates and book prizes.

A successful fortnight

The Summer School was a great success and I hope it will become an annual event so that students each year can experience the learning and fun we have had this summer. As I walked around the school during the first week of term I was greeted by happy smiling 'Beachcombers', who couldn't wait to tell me what they have been doing. They look so confident and settled already, and this must be in part due to the confidence they gained during their two-week Summer School. As I will be teaching them all once a week during the next year I will be able to monitor their progress and build on the skills learned at Summer School.

Would I give up two weeks of my summer holidays to do this again? Of course I would. So would all the staff who were involved this year, as we really enjoyed the experience!

Editor's Note: Pupils with literacy difficulties

The author informs us that not all the students were borderline Level 4. About half were and the rest were said to be a mixture. Four of the students were definitely Level 2 and were poor readers and out of their depth with some of the chosen activities which had to be amended to cater for them. They made tremendous improvements. The rest were definite Level 3 and nowhere near Level 4 at the start of the two weeks. However, at the end they weren't far off the standard required.

The writer doesn't feel that the Literacy Hour is particularly beneficial for some children with special educational needs. Those with specific learning difficulties still need small group and individual teaching using multi-sensory methods. They need time to reflect and answer and cannot rush through a routine which appears to need speed.

However, as the article shows, the Summer School can work.

The Literacy Hour in a Mainstream Secondary School

Adapted from the work sent in by Janet Spencer and Joan Collins

*Janet Spencer and Joan Collins and other members of the Sandwell CENT Team (Curriculum Enhancement) liaised with the English Department at Alexandra High School in order to produce sample resources for a scheme of work based on **Baleen** by Josephine Croser which could be used during the Literacy Hour. The intention was that all pupils in Year 7 would be able to access the work with pupils with special educational needs using correctly adapted and differentiated texts and materials.*

The teacher's notes for this exploratory work are as follows.

This scheme of work is broadly based on techniques used in the primary schools' Literacy Hour. The Literacy Hour is the medium through which the *National Literacy Strategy* is being taught. In primary schools the Hour has a firm structure, beginning with whole class work, followed by group work and concluding with a whole class 'recap'. The group work is intended to foster a pupil's ability to work independently of the teacher so that s/he can read, write and function autonomously.

It is not intended that secondary teachers should necessarily follow the structure rigidly. It can be adapted to suit local conditions and situations. However, the broad format and its main aims of fostering pupils' independent learning in order to improve literacy should always be remembered.

The whole class sessions are intended to last for about half an hour, followed by group activities. The whole class activities are designed for the whole class to read the day's text together with the teacher. Then the teacher highlights key words, spellings, phrases and sentences for language and literacy discussion. Issues arising from these sessions can then be pursued in the small group sessions later on. It would be useful to have a flip chart or similar device to record whole class key ideas etc. so that they can be referred back to, either later in the session or during subsequent lessons.

For the small group sessions, consideration needs to be given to how the groups are put together. Usually, in the groups there will need to be a chairperson, a scribe and someone who reports back to the whole class. Sometimes the pupils will work on their own within the group, sometimes in pairs and sometimes as a whole group. Pupils will need to understand how the teacher expects them to function in their groups. They will need help in understanding what working independently means. They will need to know how they are expected to work and where all the necessary resources can be found. It may be that the teacher can perhaps suggest five things that a pupil can try before asking for help. There is time built into the first lesson when the teacher can talk about these expectations.

Resources
- As many copies of the text as possible.
- An OHP.
- OHTs of the revised text on A4 paper so that the whole group can read, brainstorm and discuss short portions of text each lesson.
- A flip chart or similar.
- As many examples as possible of stories and novels for children and adults, including fairy stories, versions of Aesop's and La Fontaine's fables and other stories with morality themes.

- Poetry.
- Examples of non-fiction for children and adults, including reference books about sea life, whales etc., and newspaper and magazine articles.
- Dictionaries, thesauruses.
- Lesson plans/worksheets/task sheets for each lesson.
- Stationery including drawing equipment and paper.

Differentiation

This will be by task, resources, grouping or outcomes.

The members of the CENT team copied the rewritten text for *Baleen* onto OHT projector sheets which were intended to be projected for reading and discussion by the class. Later when working in groups the pupils would use the actual books.

The differentiation is intended to be developed in the group time when the work is tailored to the individual pupil's needs (for example, in Lesson 1 the stories and novels chosen should reflect the reading level of the pupils in the class and the collection of texts also).

Many resources were produced such as attractively produced sheets for filling in words etc. Lesson plans were devised and an example of one is reproduced below. The activities were varied and contained work such as looking at verbs and their tenses, alliteration and the use of particular vocabulary in stories and poems.

Resources needed for every lesson
- The text - *Baleen* - two versions plus OHT.
- Examples of stories and novels (as outlined above).
- Examples of non-fiction (as outlined above).
- Dictionaries, thesauruses.

Resources for this lesson
- Texts which include descriptions of whales and how they live.

Whole class session
- Aim - finding out about whales. Pupils begin to use research techniques.
- Recap of story.
- Pupils read page three.
- Highlight words which describe whales and how they live.
- Discussion of the moral issues that arise.

Group activities
- Pupils in pairs to make up questions (based on 'How', 'What', 'Why', 'When' and 'Who') - at least five.
- Use available texts to find out answers, write down answers in sentences. Draw pictures if time.

Plenary
- Report back to build up a class resource bank about whales, with a view to possible display work.

Lesson Plan.

Joan Collins and Janet Spencer went on to work in partnership with two teachers to produce schemes of work for the *B.F.G.* by Roald Dahl and *Bill's New Frock* by Anne Fine. These schemes were produced for pupils of a wide spread of abilities including those with special educational needs and it was pointed out that there was a higher proportion of pupils with special educational needs in the *B.F.G.* group.

Examples of work for particular groups was sent such as a 'capital letter and full stop A3 sheet' which is a passage of work containing no capital letters and full stops but which is large enough to use for whole class work. Another selection of worksheets included underlining adjectives, a cloze procedure sheet of adjectives and a cloze procedure set of sentences where the pupils had to fill in the missing word at the end of the sentence. It was pointed out that pupils with learning difficulties found the completion of the adjectives cloze procedure easier if they had worked on the end closures first. It was also pointed out that some work from Key Stage 2 books were more acceptable for such pupils.

The schemes of work on the three books have been well thought out and prepared providing a structure which can be differentiated and adapted for those who cannot readily access the texts independently.

A Whole School Literacy Policy in a Mainstream Secondary School

Sue Webb and Louise Wood

Introduction

Tewkesbury School is an 11 to 18 comprehensive secondary school situated in a small market town in the north west of Gloucestershire. Currently the school has over 1400 students, but will rise to over 1800 in the next few years. The average VRQ (verbal reasoning quotient) for the ten form entry in the current Year 7 is 95.4, in Year 8 is 94.2, and in Year 9 is 96.0.

Why whole school literacy?

There was a recognition by all subject staff that the literacy demands made by the GCSE and other Key Stage 4 examinations were such that a reading age of over 14 years was necessary in order to access the papers. There was also a growing realisation that the literacy demands placed on some students outreached their reading comprehension at Key Stage 3.

It was decided that the reading comprehension age of students would be measured in order to provide baseline data and evaluate the extent of the reading difficulties of students at Key Stage 3.

The students are screened on entry through the Cognitive Abilities Test, and it was this data that was originally used to determine the cohort of students to engage in the first pilot programme of intervention. Subsequently a whole screen reading assessment has been used to quantify the reading comprehension ages of students entering Year 7.

The original data was collated in February 1998. The assessment used was the NFER-Nelson 'Group Reading Test 11', comprehension reading test. Through this procedure a cohort of some 112 students were screened in Years 8 and 9. The results obtained led the school to realise the magnitude of the problem students have when accessing reading materials:

- In Year 8, 56 were screened and 45 were found to have a reading age below 11 years.
- In Year 9, 56 were screened and 18 were found to have a reading age below 11 years.

Later in October 1998 the whole of Year 7 was screened. Of this 288 year group, 123 were reading below 11 years, which represented 43% of the year group. Further data analysis revealed that of the 123 whose reading age was below 11 years, 57 were reading at or below 9 years. In percentage terms, those students represented 20% of the whole year group.

The consensus from all staff was that there was a need for an intervention programme, but in order to be effective, every teacher had to become a teacher of literacy.

The role of the English Faculty

An obvious focal point for action was the good practice already happening in English together with a plan for targeted intervention teaching in the English curriculum.

The Head of English led her team, who taught in mixed ability groups in Years 7 and 8 through an intervention strategy, beginning mid-March 1999. The thrust is a targeted Literacy Hour for each English group each week where they concentrate upon reading, writing and spelling skills. This policy is still evolving but is known and understood by all staff, regardless of subject specialism.

English department policy
English Department Key Stage 3: Programme of Study for Literacy
Aims
- To improve the literacy skills of all pupils in KS3.
- To ensure that all pupils are taught the reading, comprehension, spelling and grammar skills they need by the end of the key stage.

Resources
- Class sets of worksheets to be kept in every English classroom.
- Sets of textbooks for each teacher.
- Book box for individual reading in every English classroom.

Programme of Study
- All KS3 pupils to have a private reading session and comprehension work every week.
- The following skills and rules to be taught by the end of the year indicated:

Punctuation
Year 7: full stops, capital letters, exclamation marks, question marks, commas, speech marks, hyphens, paragraphing.
Year 8: apostrophes, commas (further uses), colons, quotation marks, punctuating dialogue.
Year 9: semi-colons, dashes.

Grammar
Year 7: nouns, subject and object, pronouns, verbs, tenses, infinitives, adverbs, adjectives, articles, main clauses.
Year 8: tenses, comparatives, superlatives, conjunctions, prepositions, could/would/should, this/that/these/those, subordinate clauses.
Year 9: phrases, passive/active, transitive/intransitive verbs.

Spelling
Year 7: learning spellings, rules for plurals and endings, i and e, homophones.
Year 8: prefixes, suffixes, negatives, opposites, doubling letters, using 'nt'.
Year 9: difficult words.

Pupils to have checklists for these skills in books and regularly review progress. This programme of study will be taught in addition to existing schemes of work which teach skills of reading, writing for different purposes and audiences, and speaking and listening in accordance with the English National Curriculum, and the skills learnt will be used and reinforced through the schemes of work.

The end of year exams in Year 7 and Year 8 will test pupils' skills in spelling, punctuation, grammar and comprehension, as well as other skills taught in English.

Key Stage 3 Literacy Programme
In order to ensure that we deliver the English Department Literacy Programme to all Key Stage 3 pupils, please include the following in your planning and teaching:

- Weekly Literacy Hour to coincide with Learning Support withdrawal period.
- Literacy Hour to cover individual reading, comprehension and language work.
- Integrated use of Key Stage 3 Literacy Folders to cover appropriate skills in spelling, punctuation and grammar for each year group, as outlined in Key Stage 3 Literacy Programme.

- Teaching pupils how to learn spellings and regular tests.
- Assessment of literacy skills in written work.

There is in addition to the English Faculty thrust a Literacy Working Group whose function is to discuss the implementation of a Whole School Literacy Policy within departments.

Whole school policy
Rationale

Literacy could be described as the ability to recognise, understand, use and manipulate the conventions of language. Literacy competence is inextricably connected to young people's perception of themselves and can affect not only their ability to learn, but also their motivation, self-esteem and behaviour. It is essential that all pupils at Tewkesbury School have adequate literacy skills to access the National Curriculum, develop fully as young people and cope with the demands of the world outside school.

Aims of the Policy
- To identify and meet the literacy needs of all pupils.
- To provide an intervention programme to boost the basic literacy skills of Year 7 pupils with a lower reading age than their chronological age.
- To support and direct the literacy development of pupils performing at Level 3 or below at Key Stage 3.
- To develop the literacy skills of all pupils, building upon their existing skills and aiming for excellence.
- To give literacy a high profile across the curriculum and to involve all subject areas in improving the literacy standards of pupils at Tewkesbury School.

Implementation, monitoring and evaluation
- The literacy initiative to be co-ordinated and overseen by the Literacy Co-ordinator.
- A representative from each subject area to attend meetings of the Literacy Working Party to monitor progress and generate new ideas.
- All subject areas to implement the Policy and Heads of Faculty to monitor.
- Staff training to be provided to support staff in implementing the Policy.
- Baseline, midline and end of key stage testing of pupils' literacy skills to be undertaken and results evaluated and reported.

The Policy
Reading
All subject areas to:

- incorporate reading tasks into lessons where possible;
- make explicit to the pupils the reading purpose of each task, eg to skim or scan for information, to read for comprehension etc.;
- check reading accessibility levels of texts;
- provide differentiated reading materials where needed;
- ensure task is accessible and support given where reading material is deliberately demanding;
- structure reading response work clearly;
- review existing schemes of work to incorporate a range of reading related tasks;
- teach and reinforce subject-specific vocabulary and frequently used words with use of visually helpful word displays;
- build structured activities for library/ICT research into schemes of work;

- participate in INSET training to promote awareness and understanding of how to teach reading;
- enlist the help of the Learning Support Department to help where needed and allocate time for Learning Support representative to feed back information from Learning Support meetings.

Writing

All subject areas to:

- give high priority to quality of handwriting and presentation of pupils' work, to be reflected in marking schemes;
- write the title of work and date on board when appropriate, to be copied by pupils;
- require pupils to write in full sentences where appropriate;
- emphasise the importance of clarity and accuracy in all written work;
- insist on drafting and refining of written work where appropriate;
- provide pupils with writing frames to help structure and develop their work;
- teach range of writing skills and styles required by subject;
- provide opportunities for use of ICT in drafting and presenting work.

Spelling

- Accurate spelling to be encouraged at all times.
- Laminated poster of how to learn spellings to be displayed in every classroom.
- Visual displays of commonly misspelt words and subject-specific words in every classroom.
- Dictionaries and spellchecks to be available in every classroom, and pupils encouraged to use them.
- School policy on marking and correcting spellings to be implemented by Faculty.
- Subject areas to teach and test subject-specific vocabulary.
- Inter-tutor group spelling competitions to be run.

In this way the school is providing a multifaceted approach to literacy development.

The role of SEN Faculty

The SEN Faculty operates at two levels: targeting both students on the Code of Practice and those who have been identified by the reading screen.

Screening in September 1999 with Year 7 students has shown a decrease in those reading at or below 9 years of age, to 16% of the year intake of 248 students. Of this 248 students, 95 are reading below 11 years of age, representing 38% of the intake.

The SEN team withdraw students from an English period, along with the other students who are part of the reading intervention scheme. This method of organisation enables the English teacher to be working with the remaining students on aspects of their literacy development.

Additionally, some students on the Code of Practice have further lessons at other times in accordance with their individual needs. The SEN team also have a proven track record of improving students' attainments.

Teaching emphasis

A Learning Support Worker is employed by the school full-time to work with students on the reading intervention programme. The key elements of her teaching are:

- withdrawal teaching for small groups of four or five students;
- specific targets set with each student and the IEP (Individual Educational Plan) sent home;
- assessment at regular intervals, usually once a term;
- feedback discussed with students and parents.

Parental partnership

A key element of the reading intervention project is working with parents. Initially, parents are contacted if their children are to be placed on the scheme. The purpose of this initial meeting is to explain results; describe the content of the lessons their children will be having; demonstrate how important reading is at Key Stages 3 and 4; enlist a parental partnership focusing upon reading at home.

At this meeting parents are also given a practical demonstration of how children can read yet not comprehend. Issues are discussed such as how to read with their child using 'Power Reading' methods and what reading materials to use. Some parents are not, however, in a position to read at home, so the assistant provides additional help at school.

Power Reading approach to reading at Key Stage 3
Power Reading

Strong reading comprehension skills are the basis for success in all subject areas. You can help your children develop these skills with Power Reading. Power Reading is a technique that will help your children become better readers by increasing both reading comprehension and listening comprehension skills. A Power Reading session takes only about 15 minutes.

Here's how to do it:

1. **Read to your child.**
Read aloud to your child for five minutes. (Be sure that the book from which you are reading is at your child's reading level.) Pronounce words carefully and clearly, and make appropriate pauses for full stops and commas.

2. **Listen to your child read.**
Have your child continue reading the same book aloud (he/she should begin at the point where you stopped reading). Remind your child to take it slowly and read so what he/she is saying makes sense. (That's why oral reading is so important - it's setting an example for your child.) Caution: Do not stop and correct your child while he/she is reading. If he/she stumbles on a word, make a note of it and go back later.

3. **Ask questions about the material that was read.**
Check how well your child was listening and reading by asking general questions about the material you read aloud and the material he/she read aloud. Talk about his/her responses; share ideas.

Hold a Power Reading Session with your child as often as possible. It's an excellent way to improve reading skills and an excellent way to demonstrate the importance you place on reading.

(Lee Canter, *Homework without tears*)

A key element of the school is to keep parents informed. To this end all progress and difficulties are discussed in a two-way process. Open access for consultation is provided at all times. A booklet is produced which is used in parental INSET sessions.

Primary-secondary partnerships

An important element of the scheme is a two-way flow of communication between partner primary schools and Tewkesbury School. The purpose of termly meetings are to:

- share the practice of the implementation of the literacy scheme;
- share good practice by arranging mutual observations;
- identify particular areas of literacy where improvement is most needed and work towards achieving this.

The results

The overall target of the reading intervention project is to raise reading comprehension ages to 11.0 years for Year 7 students and to 12.0 years for Years 8 and 9 students.

In total 73 students have passed through the intervention scheme since it began 12 months ago. The numbers of students have been of equal gender split. During the three months between December 1998 and March 1999 the results showed that in Year 8 there was an average increase of 12 months in reading comprehension age, with only two students deteriorating in their scores, one student by one month and the other by 23 months, due to an exclusion and social problems.

In the summer of 1999 only ten students remained in the scheme as they had not reached a reading age of 12.0 years.

An analysis of the data, up to June 1999, revealed the following:

- In Year 9 the first cohort of 14 students made an average increase of some 21 months in reading age (from February 1998 to June 1999) ranging from + 40 months to + 6 months.
- In Year 8 the first cohort of 19 students made an average increase of some 27 months (from February 1998 to June 1999) ranging from + 66 months to +4 months.
- In Year 7 the first cohort of 29 students made an average increase of some 22 months (from January 1999 to June 1999) ranging from + 40 months to -16 months (one student).

The first cohort of students who went through the scheme in the Autumn Term 1998 and did not have withdrawal help again were retested in March 1999. The results showed evidence of continued progress. Of those nine students five showed improvements ranging up to 26 months whilst three showed a deterioration up to 11 months.

Conclusion

The school has taken on board the implications of the reading comprehension results and is now actively seeking a whole school intervention policy, where every teacher is a teacher of literacy. This is an evolving policy which requires continued support for all departments in terms of INSET requirements and it also requires the commitment of the SMT (Senior Management Team) and the Headteacher in order to allow money and time to be devoted to it.

There are three main issues which are being addressed. These are:

- The comprehension of texts by students, across Key Stages 3 and 4, is demanding. Teachers need to know the readability of their texts and the reading levels of students. With this information they can make informed decisions upon how much differentiation is required.
- Teachers need to understand the complexity of the vocabulary they are expecting students to take on board, and plan how they will enable students to access this.
- All skills taught in isolation need to have relevance to the larger curriculum on offer, if they are to be internalised by students and transferred. This transference of skills is essential if the skills are to be truly mastered.

(For further information contact Sue Webb or Louise Wood, Tewkesbury School, Ashchurch Road, Tewkesbury, Gloucestershire GL20 8DF or E-mail at: swebb@tewkessch.gloucs.uk).

Recommended reading

Barclay, I. (1998) 'Improving boys' literacy' in *Basic Skills* (Summer issue).

Canter, Lee (1987) *Homework without tears,* Harper Perennial.

Dyster, S. and Lake-Grange, L. (1999) 'Can parents play a part in Secondary schools?' in *Basic Skills* (Spring issue).

Frater, G. (1997) 'Improving boys' literacy' in *Basic Skills* (Summer issue).

What works in Secondary Schools (1997) Basic Skills Agency.

PART THREE: SUPPORTING THE LITERACY HOUR

This section contains articles from those who visit schools and give advice and support and those who have undertaken research into the effect of the Literacy Hour on pupils with special educational needs. It begins with a description of a research project undertaken by Chris Smith and Helen Whiteley. One hundred and one teachers responded to a questionnaire and it is interesting that many of their responses mirror those sent in for this publication. There is optimism but there are also words of caution. The authors intend to investigate teachers' views on the Literacy Hour in more detail in the future.

An independent SEN Consultant and a freelance OfSTED Inspector give slightly differing views of how schools are tackling the *National Literacy Strategy*. Dyslexia is covered through Dorothy Smith's chapter on making sure that the needs of dyslexic pupils are known and catered for, and a joint article about 'teacher-friendly materials' which can be used for pupils with mild to moderate dyslexia. The authors examine phonic teaching through a research project. Rita Silvester gives advice about using additional adults in the Literacy Hour. Her ideas and suggestions comes from the work of one LEA's working party. There is a summary of Leicester's Support Service's booklet which supports teachers working with SEN pupils and Malcolm Garner gives advice about pupils with hearing impairment.

As the introduction to this book has described, this section ends with the description and results of another research project undertaken by Mike Johnson (Manchester Metropolitan University) and Lindsay Peer (British Dyslexia Association).

There is a pot-pourri of articles in Part Three which, it is hoped, will contain at least something of interest for everyone.

Teachers' Experiences of the Literacy Hour with Children with 'Special Difficulties'

Chris D. Smith and Helen E. Whiteley

In this article we report some of the findings of a survey we undertook in early 1999 of teachers' experiences of the first term of teaching the Literacy Hour. The survey is described fully in Smith and Whiteley (in press), but here we focus on the section of the survey which asked about children with 'special difficulties' - a term deliberately chosen neither to exclude nor include specific groups of children. In choosing the term we thus hoped to receive some feedback on various groups of children, including gifted children. In practice, however, 'special difficulties' was almost always taken to mean SEN.

We were concerned to determine whether the Literacy Hour was generally working equally well for all children and whether the specified small group and whole class sessions within the Literacy Hour worked equally well with all children. In all, we asked six questions - the last of which was open-ended - specifically on children with 'special difficulties'. There was also space for 'General comments' and there were open-ended questions elsewhere in the questionnaire, where answers might refer to SEN children.

The questions in the 'special difficulties' section were as follows:

- *Was the Literacy Hour equally effective for all children?*
  (YES/NO)
- *How effective was the Literacy Hour for children with literacy difficulties?*
  (circle) (Very effective/Effective/Neither/Ineffective/Very ineffective)
- *Is the Literacy Hour a help or a hindrance to working with children with literacy difficulties?*
  (please tick) (Help/Hindrance/Neither)
- *Does the small group session work better or worse with such children?*
  (please tick) (Better/Worse/Neither)
- *Does the whole class session work better or worse with such children?*
- (please tick) (Better/Worse/Neither)
- *Are there any other aspects of the structure of the Literacy Hour which differentially affect children with literacy difficulties?*
  (please specify)

In early January 1999 seven copies of a questionnaire were sent to the headteacher of each primary school in Blackpool, Chorley and Preston in Lancashire with a request that a copy be given to each teacher in each school year. The questionnaire sought to obtain details of the training and preparation teachers had received for the introduction of the Literacy Hour, but it was primarily concerned with teachers' experiences of the first term of teaching it - including their views on children with 'special difficulties'.

One hundred and three replies were received, but two were discarded. The results, therefore, come from 101 replies, but percentages are used where not all respondents answered a particular question, as follows:

Was the Literacy Hour equally effective for all children?

64.4% ticked YES: 35.6% ticked NO. Thus about one-third of the teachers felt that the Literacy Hour, which is supposed to benefit all children equally, did not do so.

How effective was the Literacy Hour for children with literacy difficulties?

Responses to this question were scored numerically, from 1 = 'Very effective' to 5 = 'Very ineffective'. A mean score of 2.95 was obtained, indicating a small shift towards the 'ineffective' end of the scale compared to the score of 3.10 on a seven-point scale, which had been obtained from an earlier question asking about the effectiveness of the Literacy Hour in general. Taken at face value the small difference between these figures is encouraging, but the figure of 2.95 on a five-point scale is towards the 'ineffective' end of the scale whereas 3.10 on a seven-point scale was towards the 'effective' end. In addition, the question asks about literacy difficulties rather than SEN children and was open to respondents who had ticked YES in response to the previous question. Strictly speaking, all this is inconclusive, but we are strongly tempted to interpret it as showing clearly that the Literacy Hour is less effective for children with special difficulties than it is generally - a conclusion which is supported by most of our other results.

Is the Literacy Hour a help or a hindrance to working with children with literacy difficulties?

The question was scored by giving scores of 2 to 'Help', 0 to 'Hindrance' and 1 to 'Neither'. The results here were interesting in that there was a clear difference between Key Stage 1 and Key Stage 2 teachers. Reception teachers gave a mean score of 1.10 - ie they felt that the Literacy Hour was slightly more of a help than a hindrance with children with literacy difficulties - and teachers in Years 1 and 2 with a mean score of 1.06 clearly felt the same. For both Year 3-6 and Year 5-6 teachers the mean score was 0.74, suggesting that for older children with literacy difficulties the Literacy Hour is felt to be hindering rather than helping.

It is worth noting that Key Stage 1/Key Stage 2 differences have been reported elsewhere. Smith and Whiteley (in press) found that Key Stage 1 teachers found the Literacy Hour to be easier to implement than Key Stage 2 teachers, while Fisher (1999) reported that Key Stage 1 children made more progress as a result of the Literacy Hour than Key Stage 2 children.

Does the small group session work better or worse with such children?

Here the scoring was 0 = 'Better' and 2 = 'Worse'. The mean scores across the school years ranged only from 0.57 to 0.64, so no Key Stage 1/Key Stage 2 difference was apparent and the small group sessions were generally regarded as working 'better' with children with special difficulties.

Does the whole class session work better or worse with such children?

Here the mean scores also had a narrow range - from 0.83 to 1.00 - with no trend across school years and a general view that the whole class session works less well than the small group sessions.

Are there any other aspects of the structure of the Literacy Hour which differentially affect children with literacy difficulties?

Sixty-eight of the 101 respondents wrote an answer to this open-ended question. Many points were made and answers sometimes contradicted each other. Common negative themes which emerged were:

- For children with special difficulties the level of the Literacy Hour is too high/too fast, so that children are often given 'holding activities' and may gradually get further behind and increasingly isolated.
- Many teachers commented on the need for individual support for such children and the adverse consequences of lack of support.

- Children with special difficulties need to be differentiated according to the nature of their difficulties and need to be set in groups according to ability.
- The first 30 minutes of the Literacy Hour (the whole class shared text/word/sentence work) was generally too difficult.

However, there were positive comments on these points, too:

- With adequate support the Literacy Hour can be made to work for children with special difficulties.
- Differentiating groups according to difficulties and abilities also works.
- With support and differentiation, even the first 30 minutes can be made to work.

The 'General Comments' section of the questionnaire

Half a page of the questionnaire was left for general comments. Seventy-six of the 101 respondents made comments and often wrote more than half a page. The comments varied considerably, but the balance of the comments was clearly positive. In the order of the frequency with which they were mentioned, the main themes which emerged from the comments were:

- The Literacy Hour is too prescriptive, inflexible and demanding.
- It is not suited to classes with children with a large range of abilities. It is very difficult to find tasks that are at the right level for all the children in the class. Several respondents commented that the higher ability children gain most.
- It is not suited equally to all year groups. This point is confirmed by some aspects of the data, as has been mentioned. One upper junior teacher complained of the Literacy Hour's 'infant practices'.
- Children generally enjoyed the Literacy Hour. We did not ask about children's attitudes and were somewhat surprised to hear that 'children are very positive', 'children prefer it to English lessons' and that it 'has increased enjoyment, including in boys', amongst other comments. One respondent attributed this to the clear structure of the Literacy Hour.
- There was insufficient emphasis on writing.

The second of these themes is clearly of interest here and there were many comments specifically about SEN children, including:

- *'I am optimistic that it will raise standards and it does "pull up" some SEN children. For those with Statements, funding for additional in-class support is needed.'*
- *'The Literacy Hour does not cater for children with special needs or the more able.'*
- *'I am stunned by its success... we have 47% special needs... our OfSTED was highly successful... we were able to allocate £15,000 from our budget for this... teachers and support staff (even the caretaker made "wedges") have invested hours of work to make resources at home.'*
- *'Tends to cater for the majority "middle" band of children. Whole class work often does not allow for children at higher and lower levels of ability to be stretched. It is difficult for many children to get the most support from the group work without additional adult support.'*
- *'Literacy Hour caters for the middle ability band. Whole class work does not cater for higher and lower ability children (no matter how we've tried).'*
- *'The average and above average pupils appear to be benefiting from the Hour.'*

The comment on the differential effect of the Literacy Hour on different year groups was also found for SEN children, as indicated above, but there were neither comments nor data to relate enjoyment or writing to SEN children.

Conclusions

The literature on SEN children and the Literacy Hour is still sparse, but our results reflect both what the literature predicted would happen and what has actually happened. For example, Stainthorp (1999) predicted that children with specific difficulties in literacy will make progressively slower progress, which is what our results seem to reflect.

Similarly, in the abstract to their paper Johnson and Peer (1999) report from interviews with teachers that 'pupils with SEN were being supported to *complete* rather than *engage* with tasks set' (our italics). They also found concerns about word level work, teaching methods and the need for support. However, they also reported that teachers felt that SEN children were more confident, contributed effectively in whole class work and had enhanced self-esteem. This was found after less than a term and a half of the Literacy Hour and is very different from Jones (1999), who withdraws SEN children from the whole class sessions, because 'they lack the self-esteem and confidence to react appropriately in these sessions' (p.10).

The balance of both opinion and evidence would seem to be that the view that the Literacy Hour should work equally well with all children and should benefit all children equally is facile and over-optimistic. However, as one of our teachers put it, 'the Literacy Hour needs to be allowed to evolve'. Evolution will have occurred already and we intend to sample shortly and in more detail teachers' experiences of the Literacy Hour with children with special difficulties.

References

Fisher, R. (1999) *The National Literacy Strategy: evidence from small schools*. Paper presented at The British Psychological Society Education Section Conference. University of Greenwich. November 1999.

Johnson, M. and Peer, L. (1999) *The national Literacy Hour and pupils with SEN: an investigation in two LEAs*. Paper presented at The British Psychological Society Education Section Conference. University of Greenwich. November 1999.

Jones, J. (1999) 'The implementation of the National Literacy Strategy: a response to Stainthorp.' *The Psychology of Education Review*, 23 (1), 9-10.

Smith, C. D. and Whiteley, H. E. (in press) *Developing literacy through the Literacy Hour: a survey of teachers' experiences*. Reading.

Stainthorp, R. (1999) 'The big national experiment: questions about the National Literacy Strategy'. *The Psychology of Education Review*, 23 (1), 3-8.

Correspondence

Dr Chris D. Smith, Department of Psychology, University of Central Lancashire, Corporation Street, Preston, Lancashire PR1 2HE.
Tel: 01772 893436/893420   Email: c.d.smith@uclan.ac.uk   Fax: 01772 892925

Some Personal Thoughts about the *National Literacy Strategy* from an Independent SEN Consultant

Veronica Birkett

Prior to my current work as an independent SEN consultant and trainer I was an advisory teacher with a support service. At present I am also employed by individual schools, on short-term contracts, helping SENCOs set up effective systems to support their role. This includes assessing and helping to devise appropriate Individual Education Plans (IEPs) for pupils at Stages 2-5 on the Code of Practice. This article is based on my observations, impressions and discussions with SENCOs, Literacy Co-ordinators and teachers in local schools and also with teachers from many parts of the country who attend courses that I have organised relating to the *National Literacy Strategy*. As a result, I have been able to gain a wide perspective of thoughts and feelings on the subject. The views offered here are personal ones and, of course, only reflect my interpretation of the current situation.

Impressions of the Literacy Hour and pupils with special educational needs

In general, it seems that teachers are beginning to welcome the Literacy Hour for the majority of their pupils. It provides a national framework which ensures all aspects of literacy are covered. Many of the initial doubts and fears which inevitably accompany the introduction of any radical change in schools are diminishing. The results of the summer SATs were encouraging and the recent introduction of the Additional Literacy Support (ALS) should ensure a further rise in standards. However, the progress of pupils with SEN continues to be a cause for concern and in my view the Literacy Hour has meant that provision for such pupils is often inadequate and under-funded.

The introduction of the Code of Practice, in 1993, was a positive move for pupils with SEN. It introduced a consistent approach throughout the nation, and ensured that all schools took measures to identify pupils and took some action on their behalf. This 'action' led to a huge increase of pupils who were provided with Statements. They needed to be provided with IEPs, placed at lower stages on the Code and given work specific to their needs. Statements often came with the provision of a Learning Support Assistant (LSA) for a set number of hours to work with a pupil on a particular programme of work set out in the IEP. Pupils placed at lower stages on the Code of Practice may also have been given extra help using LSAs. This help, especially in the primary sector, was usually offered within English and maths lessons. Thus the teacher was able to give more time to the remainder of the class. On the whole, schools felt that the introduction of the Code of Practice improved provision for their pupils with SEN.

The Introduction of the *National Literacy Strategy*

It is widely accepted that the needs of pupils with SEN were not adequately addressed when the NLS framework made its first appearance. It was some months before Section 4 (which takes account of the needs of pupils with SEN) was added to the Framework. However, not all teachers found the suggestions helpful and others, I have found, have never been informed of the existence of Section 4.

Now the Literacy Hour is well established, many teachers feel that the whole class shared reading and writing sessions are beneficial. By using differentiated questions etc. they are able to meet the needs of most pupils in the class. More problems are found in the management of the work at class word level. For example, it is felt that many Key Stage 2 pupils with SEN, who should be working on targets set for pupils in Key Stage 1, are being introduced to work in this session which is too challenging and actually causes great confusion.

Many teachers in Key Stage 2 feel inadequately trained to deal with the needs of the SEN pupils within the context of the Literacy Hour. Many of the familiar tried and tested SEN resources are now lying gathering dust in cupboards. The use of second chance reading schemes, phonic tapes and programmes of precision teaching and all the other strategies which before the onset of the Literacy Hour were widely used appear to have been abandoned. This is because these resources usually need the support of an additional adult.

The use of Learning Support Assistants and the Literacy Hour

Additional Literacy Support which is designed for pupils who have achieved Level 2c or 1 in the Key Stage 1 SATs has recently been introduced to schools. It has been introduced by the DfEE in an effort to ensure their target of 80% of 11 year-olds achieving a Level 4 in English in 2002 is achieved. In many schools, this has meant that those LSAs, who were previously available to support pupils with SEN in the independent sessions of the Literacy Hour, are now trained providers of the ALS. They are no longer available in their previous capacity. As a consenquence of this situation, teachers have Literacy Hour support with below average pupils who are the focus of the ALS, but the very pupils most in need of support may not be receiving any support at all. Unpaid and untrained parents are sometimes asked to fill this gap. However, parents might resent the fact that they are working without payment whilst Learning Support Assistants are being paid for similar work. There are certain areas of the country or certain schools where parents are unable to give this commitment. There are also instances where pupils with Statements are finding that their allocated LSAs are working with the ALS in the mornings and so are only available for individual Statement support in the afternoons. At this time of day, the pupils are generally less receptive to learning and often they are withdrawn from subjects other than literacy or numeracy. This means that these pupils are not receiving their entitlement to a 'broad balanced' curriculum.

This problem could be resolved by employing additional LSAs to work in the mornings so that literacy and numeracy can continue to be supported. But the ALS is set to run for two terms and the trained LSAs might find they were out of a job at the end of this period of time if other LSAs were also employed.

Conclusion

I feel that the Literacy Hour has done little for pupils with SEN and very careful consideration needs to be given to find a satisfactory way forward for them. The Government policy on inclusion means more and more pupils may be included in mainstream schools so it is crucial that these problems are addressed and schools are given some solutions. I am sure it was not the Government's intention to raise standards for most to the detriment of pupils with SEN but at the moment it appears that this is actually just what is happening.

The SENCO's Resource: The Use of Additional Adults in the Literacy Hour

Rita Silvester

The introduction of the Literacy Hour provided Derby City LEA with the opportunity to convene a literacy forum focusing on the needs of SEN pupils. Membership of the forum comprised representatives from the Educational Psychology Service, Special Needs Support Service, Literacy Consultant, Adviser with responsibility for Literacy, and SEN Adviser.

The forum was established to bring together viewpoints, information and cross-service knowledge on the impact of the Literacy Hour on SEN pupils in mainstream and special schools. Information was then collated into advice, which in turn formed part of a wider resource file for SENCOs.

With the introduction of the Literacy Hour, many teachers felt the additional adults in their room needed their roles renegotiating and defining. As an authority, Derby upholds the principle of inclusion. Its advice to schools is to move away from small group withdrawal work outside the classroom for SEN pupils during the Hour. The following is a compilation of best practice when liaising, planning and working with additional adults to ensure the needs of pupils are met. The additional adults referred to are teachers from SENSS (the Special Educational Needs Support Service) but the guidelines could also be applied to visiting speech therapists.

Four key questions were posed and then answered.

1. What is the role of the class teacher in working with the ECO (Education Care Officer) during the Literacy Hour?
The ECO makes an important contribution to facilitating the children's learning, and is highly effective in enabling children to access the Literacy Hour. As such he/she should have a significant input into the planning and delivery of this time.

It is the responsibility of the class teacher therefore to ensure that:

- the ECO is clear about his or her responsibilities in the classroom during this time;
- they provide regular opportunities for planning and discussion of the content of the Hour;
- they encourage and value the work of the ECO by providing positive feedback;
- they make sure the ECO knows the learning and support implications of the pupil's special need within the Literacy Hour and are aware of IEP targets set;
- the class teacher makes clear and realistic requests of the ECO;
- the children know the ECO's focus in the session.

At the start of any lesson good practice would give an opportunity for teacher and ECO to agree on:

- who will work with whom;
- who will delegate the tasks;
- when the ECO will intervene and when they will observe;
- how to use differentiated material;
- who will be responsible for resources;
- what to do if a child becomes disruptive and to be aware of existing strategies and management techniques.

2. What is the role of additional adults from outside agencies eg SEN support staff during the Literacy Hour?

The *National Literacy Strategy* provides an opportunity to develop the planned integration of the contribution made by additional adults. The following suggestions enhance inclusive practices during this time.

Teachers need to access the support teachers expertise through:

Planning:

- joint planning and the selection of texts;
- timetable liaison with ECO/SENCO;
- provide and/or suggest suitable resources;
- share assessments with teachers;
- work with teachers to write IEPs linked to literacy objectives or to appropriate behaviour during the segments of the Hour;
- advise on effective ways to make the Literacy Hour meaningful to particular children.

During the Literacy Hour they may be involved in:

- team teaching;
- working with the child and the ECO;
- supporting children's participation in class sessions - first half-hour and plenary;
- reinforcing or prefacing texts and/or skills to be taught;
- working with a group during the 20-minute session;
- carrying out IEP work;
- differentiating activities for the child being supported.

Support teachers could provide professional development in schools by:

- offering training opportunities for teachers, ECOs, and parents;
- sharing subject knowledge with teachers, eg phonics, listening skills, differentiation of questioning, classroom and/or behaviour management, collaborative skills, assessment and monitoring activities.

3. What is the role of the ECO who is deployed to work with a specific child with Statemented needs?

Good practice should ensure that:

- pupils are given access to as much of the Literacy Hour as possible keeping withdrawal activities to an absolute minimum;
- the child's IEP is delivered;
- the pupil is encouraged to be as independent as possible;
- the pupil learns some new skills or improves those already learnt;
- co-operative working practices are fostered;
- the pupil can gain some success.

Finally, research has shown that children have gained significant benefits from opportunities to work with the ECO outside of the Literacy Hour doing preparation, and top-up work. As little as five or ten minutes rehearsal or reinforcement work later that day or prior to the next Literacy Hour has had a substantial impact on levels of achievement.

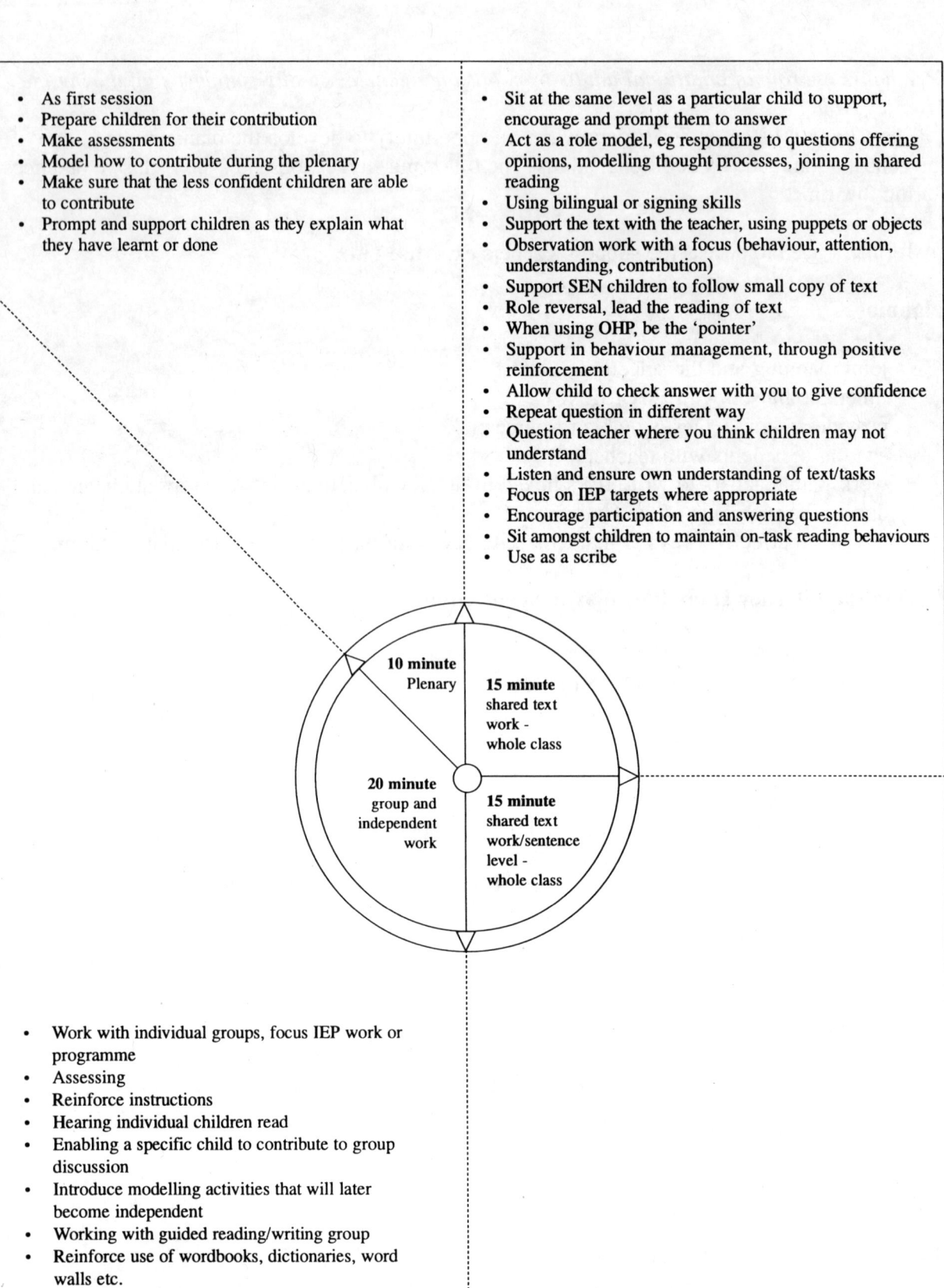

- As first session
- Prepare children for their contribution
- Make assessments
- Model how to contribute during the plenary
- Make sure that the less confident children are able to contribute
- Prompt and support children as they explain what they have learnt or done

- Sit at the same level as a particular child to support, encourage and prompt them to answer
- Act as a role model, eg responding to questions offering opinions, modelling thought processes, joining in shared reading
- Using bilingual or signing skills
- Support the text with the teacher, using puppets or objects
- Observation work with a focus (behaviour, attention, understanding, contribution)
- Support SEN children to follow small copy of text
- Role reversal, lead the reading of text
- When using OHP, be the 'pointer'
- Support in behaviour management, through positive reinforcement
- Allow child to check answer with you to give confidence
- Repeat question in different way
- Question teacher where you think children may not understand
- Listen and ensure own understanding of text/tasks
- Focus on IEP targets where appropriate
- Encourage participation and answering questions
- Sit amongst children to maintain on-task reading behaviours
- Use as a scribe

10 minute Plenary

15 minute shared text work - whole class

20 minute group and independent work

15 minute shared text work/sentence level - whole class

- Work with individual groups, focus IEP work or programme
- Assessing
- Reinforce instructions
- Hearing individual children read
- Enabling a specific child to contribute to group discussion
- Introduce modelling activities that will later become independent
- Working with guided reading/writing group
- Reinforce use of wordbooks, dictionaries, word walls etc.
- Reinforce independent working strategies
- Prepare children for following week's shared text
- Praise children as they work
- Last two minutes prepare for plenary

- As above

What can additional adults do during each part of the Literacy Hour?

The *National Literacy Strategy* and Pupils with Dyslexia

Dorothy Smith

Pupils with dyslexia learn differently from other pupils and have distinct problems which can be pinpointed. However, being given the label 'dyslexic' does not mean that all these pupils have similar learning needs.

Dyslexia is constitutional in origin and it results in differences in various aspects of information processing, both visual and auditory, and it causes particular difficulties in literacy skills. These difficulties should not be thought of as deficiencies but as differences in learning. This, therefore, should lead to different methods of teaching. Usually reading is easier to acquire than spelling.

Teachers have to organise and teach an appropriate programme of work and then allow dyslexic pupils to succeed. Dyslexic pupils may have a Statement of Special Educational Need or may have been placed on one of the Code of Practice stages. They most probably will have an IEP (Individual Education Plan) which should set out their learning needs.

Because the *National Literacy Strategy* is well organised and well structured it should suit pupils with dyslexia. Dyslexic pupils are entitled, as are their peers, to take part in the Literacy Hour. They can benefit from and participate well in the text level work with the Literacy Hour. They can cope well within the shared reading and shared writing session and they can take their part in the plenary. But there can be an organisational issue with word level work and in order that dyslexic pupils gain the optimum from the Literacy Hour there are many points to be answered and issues to be discussed.

1. *Make sure that you have some prior knowledge of pupil's dyslexic literacy difficulties.*

- Pupils might have problems on the auditory side with learning to read and spell. These might show in difficulties with:

  - phonological awareness;
  - auditory discrimination;
  - auditory memory;
  - concentration;
  - listening and speaking;
  - word finding/retrieval.

- Pupils might have problems on the visual side with learning to read and spell. These might show in difficulties with:

  - visual discrimination;
  - visual memory;
  - sequencing;
  - organisation;
  - fine motor skills.

- Take into account the individual differences in pupils when you plan for the Literacy Hour. Identify and diagnose the problems the dyslexic pupils experience. If you find this difficult ask the SENCO for advice and help. Or there may be Advisory and Support staff or Educational Psychologists within the LEA who will assess a particular child and offer information and advice about problem areas and programmes of work. The earlier the pupils are identified the better. Even if young pupils subsequently are found not to be dyslexic but have developmental delay the extra support will have been most beneficial to their literacy acquisition.

2. *Try to understand that dyslexic pupils have strengths which can be built upon and put to good advantage.*

- Pupils might have strengths in:

    - competent cognitive abilities in the average to above average range;
    - good conceptual understanding;
    - satisfactory expressive language with a wide range of spoken vocabulary;
    - satisfactory receptive language;
    - interesting imagination.

- Provide opportunities for the pupils to demonstrate these strengths. Celebrate these and let others (non-dyslexic pupils) realise that you feel there is merit in other areas rather than just in reading and spelling.

3. *Examine all the organisational issues that might arise.*

- Make sure that those dyslexic pupils who have been identified are known to those adults who work within the Literacy Hour. This is important because if adults inadvertently ask pupils who are dyslexic to attempt something outside their capabilities loss of self-esteem can result. Also it is important not to judge dyslexic pupils by their literacy attainments as this might look as if they have low intellectual abilities.
- If the classes are 'setted' (eg three teachers and two classes) look carefully at where the dyslexic pupils are placed. It would be hoped that there is some flexibility where this is concerned. If dyslexic pupils are always placed in groups according to their literacy attainments they will not use their better language and conceptual skills to the best of their advantage. As has been stated text level work will be profitable and many dyslexic pupils will shine in question and answer sessions. However, it is possible that dyslexic pupils sometimes may need to work in a smaller group which works at a slower pace or even occasionally individually, especially if this meets the requirements of the Statement. Flexibility of organisational issues will be needed.
- If the pupils are organised into ability groupings within the mixed ability class it is important to determine how these abilities are identified. Are these by cognitive ability, reading or spelling attainment, or by expressive language? If groups are organised through reading and spelling attainment dyslexic pupils will not work on higher language or conceptual understanding tasks at their own levels.
- It is important to look into ways that the dyslexic pupil can move between groups if this is felt to be helpful. This might be difficult but is probably the best way to work. Dyslexic pupils will then have the best of all worlds. They can work with their ability-equals for some parts of the Hour and with a lower attainment set for others.

4. *Examine the issues of teaching programmes.*

- If dyslexic pupils are working on specialised teaching programmes you should work out if these can be incorporated into the Literacy Hour or whether they have to be additional to the work of the Literacy Hour. (These programmes are those such as 'Alpha to Omega',

'Attack', 'Toe by Toe', 'Phonological Awareness Training', 'Beat Dyslexia' or 'Spelling Made Easy'.) Dyslexic pupils often need a multi-sensory approach to acquire competent literacy skills and as these have to be cumulative and taken in small steps then, wherever possible, these should be used. But sometimes it is best to give these at another time or maybe some of the programme can be used within the word level work. These programmes encourage independence of learning and promote self-esteem.

- Make sure the specialised programmes link to the *National Literacy Strategy* objectives. If we examine the structure of such programmes it can be seen that the learning tasks fit somewhere within the NLS objectives but not in the same order. However, the NLS does not have to be followed rigidly.

- Make sure the targets on the IEP fit with NLS objectives. An additional point to be considered is should the NLS objectives be used for the IEP or should the requirements of the dyslexic pupils come first? The latter seems the most sensible approach. It is possible to make a detailed diagnostic assessment of strengths and weaknesses and then to state these as objectives or targets. Under these it can be noted where these match the objectives within the NLS. In this way it can be seen if the particular target is within the correct stage or level for the age-range of the pupil.

- Use structured reading schemes to monitor pupils' reading. Big Books, poems, parts of books and other reading materials often form the basis of the text level work but all pupils, not just dyslexic pupils, still need to read widely. Many current reading schemes are modern, attractive, fairly exciting and amusing as far as they can be with limited vocabulary. They are structured because they are either teaching a store of core words or because they have a phonic basis. Reading schemes can still form the basis of home-school reading links and often within schools there are peer tutoring groups or adult volunteers who hear readers.

- Ensure that learning is cumulative. This requires that there are plenty of opportunities for:

  - over-learning - using a variety of ways to teach the same thing;
  - repetition - lots of practice;
  - revision - revisiting items taught previously;
  - multi-sensory - simultaneously using all the senses for learning, auditory, oral, visual, tactile, kinaesthetic.

- Provide sufficient time. Adapt the pace of learning within the teaching programmes.
- Provide support for the dyslexic pupil's poor memory. In this case visual cues, checklists of instructions, diagrams, charts etc. can be given.
- Don't forget that other literacy work outside the Literacy Hour can and should be organised. Not all reading, spelling and writing will occur during one hour per day. Remember to organise any individual support which might be part of the Statement.

5. *Examine the issues of learning styles.*

- Plan and accommodate the different learning styles encountered by the dyslexic pupil within the Literacy Hour. It is important to have these identified. For example, some dyslexic pupils find auditory processing very difficult and cannot listen for a length of time and then recall what was read or said. Repetition of information may be needed. Visual clues may have to be given.
- When planning for the Literacy Hour take into account the slower pace of pupils with dyslexia. The pace of the NLS seems quite rapid but items taught are reinforced. Dyslexic pupils may need extra reinforcement, either at home or with other adults at other times in the day. It is important not to teach a skill before the dyslexic child is ready (eg phonics

cannot be taught before phonological awareness is well established, speech marks cannot make sense unless sentences are understood).

- Plan for over-learning, repetition, rehearsal and revision. Because of the slower pace of the dyslexic pupil repetition etc. is needed. The NLS core words for reading can be practised daily through probes (precision testing). This takes a minute or two only. Five words for spelling retention can be practised daily. The alphabet can be repeated once a day and plastic or wooden letters can be sequenced at the beginning of each word-level session. If dyslexic pupils get into the habit of a routine then over-learning becomes a habit.

6. *Examine the issues of reading and recording.*

- Plan for alternatives to reading. Are there other adults who will read to the dyslexic pupils who will then follow the text? Are story tapes used? These are excellent for over-learning. Is there a computer which has visual and auditory stories? Can the complete non-reader use some kind of symbols or Rebus approach?
- Plan a variety of ways of recording work. Use an adult scribe as often as possible for the non-writing dyslexic pupil. Sometimes dyslexic pupils need to dictate their imaginative stories or factual accounts to an adult who might then word-process these so that self-esteem is bolstered. There are many programs for PCs which enable dyslexic pupils to construct stories.
- Allow the dyslexic pupil to use the computer as much as possible. All pupils benefit from working on computers and it could be difficult to make the case for dyslexic pupils to have what might seem more than their fair share. But it pays dividends where confidence is concerned.

7. *Work <u>with</u> the dyslexic pupil.*

- Let the dyslexic pupils know that you understand their particular difficulty and explain why they have been placed into particular groupings for particular parts of the Literacy Hour.
- Explain how you will be working with them to overcome their literacy problems.
- Make sure you know and understand the aspects of learning they find difficult. Listen to them and they might tell you points that you don't actually know. Dyslexic pupils have insight to their own problems.

8. *Work with parents.*

- Involve parents as much as possible. Give them details of what you have provided for their child and what you hope to achieve from the programmes.
- Organise a home-school book where two-way information can be given.
- Only expect parents to 'teach' or work on a reading or spelling programme if they feel happy with this.

Most teachers can identify some pupils with special educational needs in their classes; most of these will know of at least one pupil with dyslexia. There may be more. Although it may seem to bring extra work to organise suitable work and to provide correct learning experiences for a few pupils it is necessary if pupils with dyslexia are to gain appropriate skills.

Teacher-Friendly Materials for Pupils with Mild to Moderate Dyslexia

Mike Johnson, Sylvia Phillips and Lindsay Peer

During the past five years there has been considerable discussion and concern relating to the rising number of pupils being given the protection of Statements of Special Educational Needs, many of whom are diagnosed as dyslexic.

The results are that:

- LEAs sometimes seek to discontinue existing Statements or are reluctant to assess for them in the first place;
- specialist services are overburdened and pupils do not get the individual attention awarded to them in the Statement;
- schools and teachers may feel abandoned;
- parents become concerned that their child's needs are not being met;
- many children with significant, but not severe needs are not being allowed the resources to meet their needs.

This has contributed to an increase in the number of appeals to the SEN Tribunal which themselves are costly in terms of both specialist time and resources.

Following the publication of the 1994 SEN Code of Practice, the then Department for Education commissioned this project to identify methods of identification and assessment of specific learning difficulties (dyslexia) and effective intervention strategies which can be used by classroom teachers and learning support assistants in mainstream schools.

The research element of the project was conducted in two phases:

Phase One:

- a literature review of available methods to inform decisions regarding which identification and intervention procedures should be trialled;
- a survey of 122 specialist teachers to identify the form of identification and intervention methods; and
- interviews with the heads of four specialist services to examine their policies and procedures on intervention strategies.

Phase Two:

- a comparative trialling and evaluation of three published schemes in 13 primary schools. This involved:
- an initial two-hour training session for class teachers and learning support assistants;
- within each school, groups of six pupils with dyslexic-type reading difficulties were identified;
- groups were taught for 10/15 minutes for a minimum of four days each week for eight weeks;
- pupils were assessed through pre- and post-tests on reading and spelling, together with follow-up interviews with pupils and staff to evaluate learning outcomes more qualitatively.

Literature

The British Dyslexia Association estimates that at least 4% of pupils (at least one in each class on average) have severe dyslexia. This also means that in each class there will be some pupils who may have mild to moderate dyslexia, which might have been overcome, had appropriate teaching methods started early enough. There may be other pupils whose literacy development is hindered by the methods normally used in infant classrooms. These could all be described as 'instructional casualties'. In all these examples there is a danger that the reasons for their difficulties may be seen as in the environment (poor homes, economic conditions, etc.) or within the child (slow learner, emotional problems, not 'settled' yet, etc.) rather than in the teaching methods. However, Project Read in the USA and more recently, in the UK, Watson and Johnston (1998) and Solity and Deaves (1999) demonstrated that successful methods with all these pupils were 'basically synthetic and multi-sensory as opposed to the analytic technology (methods) of the whole word-meaning approach' (Enfield, 1981, p.4).

In *Analytic Phonics* reading teaching starts with whole words. This was sometimes referred to as 'Look-and-Say'. The child's attention is drawn to letters and sounds within the words taught, ie *analysing* a word for sounds. Children are then taught to 'sound-out' and blend unfamiliar words, eg 'cuh-ah-tuh' for 'cat'. In the *Synthetic Phonics* method letter sounds are taught and pupils shown how they can build words from independent sounds. They learn to form words from these sounds as soon as possible.

Most phonic methods, including those in the *National Literacy Strategy*, lie somewhere between the two extremes. Synthetic phonics introduces the 44 sounds of English in an order that allows them to be combined to make up many words. Words containing letters not yet taught should not be presented for a child to read, certainly not to read aloud. Some pupils may well have lost their confidence in their ability to deal with print at all. Use of synthetic phonics can re-establish their self-confidence through its emphasis on teaching as opposed to learning.

A literature search revealed that in the USA there were several examples of teaching schemes for dyslexic pupils using 'synthetic', direct teaching methods. Early programmes were still based on individual instruction by teachers who had undergone special training. However, Margaret Smith in Texas, amongst others, made further developments resulting in a programme for group use in mainstream schools, the Multi-sensory Teaching System (MTS) (Smith, 1993). The programme is broken down into short (15-minute), self-contained lessons and what the teacher says to the pupils and their likely replies are given. Thus the scheme is fully 'scripted' with all equipment provided so that the only demands on the teacher were that s/he reads and understands the lesson ahead. It intersperses the direct teaching of phonics with that of morphology and word structure. The lessons follow the sequence and structure developed within the Orton, Gillingham and Stillman and Aylott Cox tradition. They use a multi-sensory teaching approach to maximise their effectiveness with pupils finding the attainment of literacy difficult. Pupils' progress is partly self-recorded and they are encouraged to take charge of their own learning. Because of the clarity of the scheme, teachers had no difficulty in keeping detailed notes.

It was felt that if a scheme was developed for use in the UK based on synthetic phonics combined with direct instruction, it could be used with any pupil not developing literacy easily. There would be no need for screening as these are perfectly valid techniques for teaching any child to read. Further, if a pupil taught using these multi-sensory methods did not begin to make progress there would be a clear case for him/her to be referred promptly ('fast-tracked') for specialist assessment at Stage 4 of the Code of Practice. Further, because of the structure of the scheme the teacher can make a very positive contribution to that assessment.

Survey of specialist teachers

Three hundred and seventy-one teachers who had received a specific learning difficulties (dyslexia) teaching qualification from the Manchester Metropolitan University SEN Centre, were sent a questionnaire asking them about their teaching, how they assessed the literacy skills of mainstream pupils, methods they found effective in teaching mainstream pupils and teaching dyslexic pupils in general, and the basis on which they described pupils as dyslexic.

Of the 122 who completed and returned the questionnaire 80% were employed by support services to work with pupils with specific learning difficulties (dyslexia) in mainstream schools. 52% worked with primary-age pupils, 27% worked with secondary-age pupils and 21% with both. The majority of pupils seen had a Statement of SEN and the most common basis of describing a child as dyslexic was if the Statement mentioned dyslexia. The second most frequent reason was if a pupil matched a list of common specific learning difficulties (dyslexia) characteristics. Third was diagnosis by an educational psychologist.

They listed up to ten methods they had used to teach pupils with specific learning difficulties (dyslexia) and rated each for its effectiveness, ease of use and suitability in relation to group size. There was strong agreement as to which methods were considered most easy to use and which were most effective. In total 190 methods were regarded as suitable for individuals, 160 for teaching small groups and 39 for class teaching, of which there was consensus over five. These were:

- multi-sensory approach in general;
- Violet Brand's spelling books;
- alphabet and dictionary work;
- Information Communication Technology;
- Look-Say-Cover-Write (or its variations) for learning spellings.

Interviews with Specialist Service Heads

The Heads of four Learning Support Services responsible for the delivery of support to mainstream pupils in different areas of the North-West were interviewed about their policies, practices and procedures.

There were two distinct areas of intervention: literacy-skills acquisition and curriculum access. Intervention was provided by either withdrawal tuition or in-class support. The most important features of interventions to improve the literacy skills of pupils with specific learning difficulties (dyslexia) were thought to be:

- early intervention;
- structured, multi-sensory, sequential, cumulative small steps;
- revision/over-learning;
- reinforcement;
- individualised;
- promote self-esteem;
- making learning fun;
- pupils control learning;
- help access the curriculum.

It was considered that if all pupils could follow a structured phonics/literacy programme fewer were likely to fail to learn to read.

Key findings

- The literature review identified phonological awareness as a prerequisite for all pupils when learning to read and that interventions which focus on phonics are more effective if directly related to the reading process.
- A questionnaire to specialist teachers showed that the methods they use all:
  - promote phonological awareness, ensure 'over-learning' and give time for review and attainment of mastery;
  - are based on cumulative, structured, sequential multi-sensory delivery with frequent small steps; and
  - encourage independent learning and improved self-esteem.
- In the evaluation of the three published schemes based on these principles, all produced significant gains in reading and spelling attainments and enhanced the pupils' understanding of how to learn to read.
- The most effective and accessible of these was the Multi-sensory Teaching System (MTS).
- Teaching methods for pupils who do not easily acquire literacy should:
  - be structured, sequential and multi-sensory and ensure 'over-learning';
  - provide an effective screening method to identify pupils who do not find the attainment of literacy easy and require further assessment.

Trialling the schemes

The Multi-sensory Teaching System (MTS) was evaluated alongside two sets of similar materials currently available in the UK. Each of the schemes used a multi-sensory approach and could be broken down into a series of short, carefully structured, self-contained lessons. All the equipment was provided so that the only demands on the teacher were s/he reads and understands the lesson ahead. Pupils partly self-recorded their progress and were encouraged to take charge of their own learning. Because of the clarity of the scheme, teachers found no difficulty in keeping accurate detailed notes and assessing progress. These three schemes were subsequently evaluated in Phase 2 of the project.

The results showed that over eight weeks gains in both reading and to some extend spelling attainments were achieved, even though the latter was not directly 'targeted'. Year 2 classes using MTS showed gains in reading age of nine months on the MacMillan Individual Reading Inventory and four months on the Vernon Spelling Test. The class using PAT gained two months and five months respectively. The Year 5 classes using MTS showed average gains in reading age of four months on the Neale analysis and those using one of the other schemes gains of seven months in both reading and spelling ages. The most successful of the three approaches was MTS in terms of improved reading and spelling ages (Year 2 only), self-esteem of pupils and acceptance by teachers and learning support assistants.

Follow-up interviews with both pupils and staff showed that previously failing pupils had now joined the 'success-flow' of the school. Pupils all felt that their literacy skills had improved as a result of their involvement in the project and the methods used were seen as not only acceptable but also professionally enhancing by both teachers and learning support assistants. Schools that continued to use the materials after the end of the formal evaluation period confirmed that these effects were maintained.

The evidence confirmed that the delivery of the mainstream reading curriculum in a sequential form enhanced the pupils' chances of staying in the mainstream of attainment and support previous American studies. They also provided an early indication of pupils who may have significant difficulties in learning to read and require further assessment.

Conclusions

The research identified a valid teaching technology for use in mainstream classrooms with pupils who do not find the attainment of literacy easy. It therefore provides evidence that the development and wider use of teaching packages which support reading in a sequential structured multi-sensory form will enhance the changes with mild to moderate specific learning difficulties (dyslexia) in a mainstream setting. The research did not aim to pinpoint effective materials for teaching pupils with severe dyslexia in mainstream schools. We believe firmly that such pupils need multi-professional assessment and specialist teaching from an appropriately qualified professional.

A UK version of the Multi-sensory Teaching System for reading has been developed by the project team, and includes a DfEE checklist ('Handy Hints for Primary School Teachers') to identify 'at risk' pupils, a teachers' handbook, demonstration video and teaching materials.

Bibliography

DfE (1994) *Code of Practice on the Identification and Assessment of Special Educational Needs.* London: HMSO.

DfEE (1999) *'Handy Hints for Primary Schools'*, Laminated Poster, London: DfEE.

Enfield, M. L. and Green, V. E. (1981) 'Project read', *Bulletin of the Orton Society,* Vol. 31.

Smith, M. T. (1993) *Multi-sensory Teaching System,* Publishers: MTS Forney, Texas.

Solity, J. (1998) *'An investigation into effective instructional approaches to increasing attainments in reading and to presenting difficulties'*. Unpublished paper, University of Warwick and Leverhulme Trust.

Watson, J. E. and Johnstone, R. S. (1998) *Accelerating Reading Achievement: the effectiveness of synthetic phonics.* Edinburgh: Scottish Office.

For further information contact:

Mike Johnson, Special Educational Needs Centre, Institute of Education, Manchester Metropolitan University, Didsbury, Manchester M20 2RR.
Tel: 0161 247 2060   Fax: 0161 247 6814   E-mail: M.C.JOHNSON@MMU.AC.UK
or
Lindsay Peer, Education Director, British Dyslexia Association, 98 London Road, Reading, Berkshire RG1 5AU.
Tel: 0118 966 2677   Fax: 0118 935 1927   E-mail: admin@bda-dyslexia.demon.co.uk

Note: Whilst the work referred to above was commissioned and financed by the DfEE, the opinions expressed in this report are the writers' own and do not necessarily reflect those of the DfEE.

Impressions of a Freelance OfSTED Inspector

Gill Carter

These have been taken from a wide variety of Literacy Hour arrangements whilst undertaking 15 school inspections over the past year. The categories of pupils have been diverse, ranging from those in special schools (eg deaf, PMLD, MLD, speech and language impaired) to those who could be termed underachievers in mainstream settings.

The plenary sessions where there are whole class inputs have sometimes been problematic for pupils with special educational needs who also have concentration problems. This is particularly so where no other adults are present. Schools with special units or generous adult support often withdraw pupils for the Literacy Hour to work at similar tasks to their peers but which have been differentiated to a more appropriate range and pace. The Literacy Hour is often very successful in special schools where it can be very precisely targeted.

In lots of settings there is the need for more adult support. Some schools still seem to feel insecure about breaking away from the constraints of the *National Literacy Strategy* to make individual provision for individual needs. It is crucial that there is enough time for teachers to plan the daily sessions and to provide appropriate tasks and materials.

Where the Literacy Hour has been most successful is in those schools which focus precisely on the needs of those pupils with special educational needs. The overall benefit is the range of learning opportunities which are offered and most pupils indicate that they like the time spent in the Hour. A spin-off from the work planned for the Literacy Hour is that other curriculum areas have benefited from improved differentiation. Where this has occurred the quality of teaching for those pupils with special educational needs has been enhanced.

One SEN Support Service Response

Special Needs Teaching Service, Leicester

Many LEAs have responded to the Literacy Strategy by producing 'in-house' booklets. These may have been written by the Literacy Consultants or with extra guidance and input from members of the LEA special educational needs support services. Some LEAs took the opportunity of involving teachers or surveying schools, especially if some of these took part in the pilot project.

One such LEA is Leicester. Their document is called *Access for all in the Literacy Hour* and was produced by the Special Needs Teaching Service in association with the Educational Psychology Service, Literacy Consultants, the Minority Ethnic Language and Achievement Service with support and advice from members of the Quality and Development Service within the Education Department.

Their aim in producing the booklet is based 'on promoting the inclusion of all children' and it has 'been collated to provide additional practical advice for teachers working with particular groups of children... based on good planning and classroom practice'.

Access for children with special educational needs in mainstream classes

There are five chapters. Chapter One is entitled 'Access for Children with Special Educational Needs in Mainstream Classes' and it gives advice on delivering the *National Literacy Strategy* successfully to children with differing special educational needs that may be found in mainstream schools. Therefore, there are sections covering general learning difficulties, specific learning difficulties, speech and language difficulties, behavioural difficulties, impaired hearing, partially sighted children, braillists/blind and autistic spectrum disorders. Each section is written to a common format. Usually there is a general descriptor of the particular special need with some general information and advice. Then there are sections on the four parts of the Hour with small clocks to alert the reader to whether the ideas given are concerning shared text, word and sentence level, group work or the plenary. Each practical suggestion is bullet pointed. For example, where behavioural problems are concerned the shared text and word/sentence level work ideas are:

- Prepare for sitting on the carpet by rehearsing, sitting in groups at register, milk or discussion time.
- Prepare for other routines within the Literacy Hour by practising in advance.
- Use peer support to encourage and to participate in the group activity.
- Take regard of seating position of all children, ie are they comfortable, can they see, minimise disruption for distractible pupils.
- Where additional adult support is available, use it to monitor, scan, intervene and praise.

Access for children with special educational needs in other settings

The second chapter is 'Access for Children with Special Educational Needs in Other Settings'. Its format is the same as Chapter One but the two sections deal with special schools and units and with pupils with special educational needs in pre-school settings. The authors point out that there is no statutory obligation for children under five years of age to be included in the NLS but they point out that standard good Nursery practice can be a good preparation for later lessons and can help lay secure literacy foundations. It is recognised that children with special needs 'will require more individual and small group support and some differentiation of curriculum content and pace'. This section doesn't divide into the parts of the Hour as it gives 12 suggestions concerning early reading, writing and language activities and opportunities.

Bilingual children, black Caribbean children and dual heritage children

Chapter 3 is concerned with bilingual children in the early stages of learning English and black Caribbean children and dual heritage children. These two sections give general information and then divide the Hour into its four parts and suggest activities and provide ideas about dealing with cultural differences. The author's main emphases are:

- using books that reflect pupils' experiences and backgrounds
- ensuring that all pupils understand the text particularly by focusing on the key words that carry meaning
- using buzz groups and other techniques to involve all pupils in focused oral activities.

Role of additional adults in the Literacy Hour

The fourth chapter has one page set out as a clock diagram where suggestions for the 'Role of Additional Adults in the Literacy Hour' are set out. For example, in the shared text time the extra adult might:

- sit amongst children to maintain on-task, reading behaviours
- all children to check answer with you to give confidence
- focus on IEP work.

There are many ideas given for the four sessions of the Literacy Hour and the authors stress that schools have to work out ways of ensuring that there is communication between teachers and classroom assistants, especially for planning and feedback. However, there are no ideas given here.

Interviews

The final chapter summarises a series of interviews carried out in the City's pilot schools. Teachers were asked about their thoughts on the Literacy Hour and how it might meet the needs of children with special educational needs. Lists of 'positives' and 'constraints' were given both generally and divided up as in the same format as most of the other chapters into the four areas of the Hour. As has been noted by NASEN's respondents Leicester teachers found that generally children enjoyed the Literacy Strategy, they understood what they were learning and why they were doing it, and they were pleased to demonstrate their strengths.

Obviously as the years go by LEAs will be able to draw on the working practices within their schools and update booklets such as the one written by Leicester. In this way practices can become more standardised within particular sets of circumstances. As long as there are support services for children with special educational needs children with learning difficulties and other problems will be included within the whole curriculum.

For further information contact: Janis Warren, Head of Special Needs Teaching Service, New Parks House, Pindar Road, Leicester LE3 9RN.

The Literacy Hour: Pupils with Hearing Impairment

Malcolm Garner

The Flash Ley Resource Centre, Stafford, is an Education Advisory Service for Hearing Impaired, Visually Impaired and Physically Disabled Pupils. The Hearing Impaired Service supports children with impaired hearing in mainstream schools and the pupils vary tremendously depending upon the degree of hearing loss and their previous exposure to language. Learning Support Assistants are employed to reinforce and modify language on an individual basis.

It is felt by this service that the Literacy Hour has worked to the advantage of hearing impaired children. The focus and structure relates well to the work that the teachers of the Deaf undertake. However, the pace of work may sometimes be a problem.

The service has produced a booklet which sets out suggestions for staff working with hearing impaired children within the Literacy Hour and the following points have been reproduced from this.

General notes

- All pupils with a hearing impairment should be able to join in and benefit from the Literacy Hour along with their peers.
- All hearing impaired children will rely to a greater or lesser extent on visual reinforcement. This may be in the form of lip-reading, facial expression, gesture and, for some children, sign language support. Some children will need modified or adapted materials.
- For some children who receive additional support because of their hearing loss it may be appropriate to spend some of the time in individual work in a quieter environment.

Shared text work

- In most cases it will be important for the child to sit at the front for group work with an unobstructed view of the teacher. The teacher should remember not to sit with the windows behind them as their faces will then be in silhouette. This can make lip-reading very difficult.
- When sharing a text, for example a Big Book, care should be taken not to talk to the book. Teachers must try to look and point first and then turn and speak to the group.
- If teachers need to check that the child can see clearly ask them to read something rather than asking if they can see. They will probably say 'yes' even when they can't. Similarly if teachers need to check understanding they should ask for an explanation rather than a 'yes/no' answer.
- If a Learning Support Assistant is involved in the group work, an individual smaller copy of the Big Book may be helpful so that the teacher's explanations and questions can be modified or repeated with reference to the appropriate text and illustrations.
- Children with a severe hearing impairment lack the 'incidental learning' of hearing children and, therefore, have a less well developed understanding of vocabulary and concepts. For example, they may know what a 'bus' is because they can relate the word to the object but may not know the term 'driver' because of the abstract function.
- It may be helpful for the child to have time to go through the work individually, either before or after the Literacy Hour to rehearse or reinforce key elements of vocabulary.

Additional notes for Key Stage 2

- When other children are reading shared text aloud the child with hearing impairment may not be able to follow. Try using a partner to point to the text as it is read.

- When other children are sharing their own work with the class or group they should be encouraged to stand or sit where the child with a hearing impairment can see them.
- If a radio aid is in use the microphone should be passed to the relevant speaker. This may sometimes be another child.

Plenary session

The notes regarding shared text will apply in these sessions. Below are a few additional notes on ways of making this session more accessible to the hearing impaired pupil.

- The hearing impaired pupil will often find the group discussion sessions the most difficult because they may not be able to hear all the contributions made by others in the class. A good strategy is for the teacher to repeat key points. It is likely that this strategy will benefit other children as well as the hearing impaired pupil.
- If a Learning Support Assistant is employed they may be able to note key points and reinforce them individually later.
- Teachers should try and include the hearing impaired pupil in class discussion. If done sensitively it can be a very good means of building confidence.

Focused word work and sentence work

- Despite their deafness a phonics approach is still helpful for most children with a hearing loss. However, they are likely to have significantly more difficulty than hearing children.
- A small number of pupils with more severe deafness will have considerable difficulty with a phonics approach. In such cases specialist teachers should be consulted who will be able to offer advice.
- The child may look for lip patterns to supplement what they hear and help them to discriminate sounds. It should be remembered that whilst providing vital clues, lip patterns can be very ambiguous and only convey part of the information.
- Rhyme, intonation, alliteration etc. may need additional reinforcement with repetition, explanation and visual cues.

Group and independent work

- During group work and guided text work it may be helpful for the child with a hearing impairment to be paired with a partner. Careful pairing will need to be made so that the hearing child does not 'take over'.
- Some children may need modified text for comprehension exercises. Unfamiliar vocabulary or difficult sentence construction may need explanation or prior alteration.
- Careful preparation should ensure that the child with a hearing impairment is able to successfully complete a task independently. If adult support is available it should be considered how the child can be encouraged to be less dependent.
- If a radio aid is in use teachers should remember to switch off the microphone when talking to another group. Then it must be switched back on when moving to the group with the child with a hearing impairment or when working with the whole class.
- Children with better hearing in one ear should sit with their better side nearest to the group or their partner.
- When dividing the children into groups the child with a hearing impairment should be put into a group with children of similar ability rather than in the 'special needs group' unless that is appropriate because of their ability.

Pupils with SEN and the Literacy Hour

Mike Johnson and Lindsay Peer

At the end of January 1999, the Manchester Metropolitan University (MMU) and the British Dyslexia Association (BDA) were awarded funds by the DfEE to gather data relating the access of pupils with SEN to the Literacy Hour.

This was a 'snapshot' study, the data being collected during February 1999. Manchester and Salford LEAs collaborated with the University in both the design and the execution of the project. They are both large, inner urban authorities but with a range of suburban and 'overspill' areas giving a good mixture of socio-economic groupings.

The research consisted of three parts:

- a review of selected contemporary literature
- interviews with teachers and SENCOs
- observations of Literacy Hour teaching.

The interviewers were MMU tutors and an independent dyslexia consultant. Observations were carried out by the Adviser for Literacy, Manchester LEA and the Special Educational Needs Adviser for Salford LEA. Each LEA nominated five primary schools recognised as having good practice in their literacy teaching and with at least satisfactory reports in their OfSTED inspections. Two schools in each LEA were nominated for the collection of observational data, and the other three for interviews. In the 'Observation' schools two classes were nominated in each school. One was the class taken by the Literacy Co-ordinator, the other by the SENCO. In each 'Interview' school three classes were nominated, two as above and the third to give a spread of pupils at the end of Key Stages 1 and 2. Supply cover was given so that interviews could be relaxed and the classes not disadvantaged. Each lasted about one hour.

Contemporary literature

The *National Literacy Strategy* developed from the work of the Literacy Task Force set up in May 1996 by the then Shadow Secretary of State for Education and Employment, David Blunkett. Aiming to raise the standards of literacy in English primary schools over a five to ten-year period it attracted a great deal of comment. Some was both provocative and inaccurate. '*Scots throw down literacy gauntlet*' (*Times Educational Supplement*, October 1998); '*Literacy Hour is too long*' (*Times Educational Supplement*, November 1998). The former refers to Watson and Johnston's (1998) study distinguishing between analytic and synthetic phonics; the latter to Solity et al's Early Reading Research Project (ERR) summarised in Solity, Deavers, Kerfoot, Crane and Cannon (1999).

- Watson and Johnston (op. cit.) concluded that, 'The synthetic phonics method leads to fewer underachieving children.' However, the headline quoted above sets up a 'man of straw' as the NLS advocates exclusive use of neither analytic nor synthetic phonics at the word level. Watson and Johnston state that, 'Children have to be shown that the sequence of the phonemes in the spoken word maps on to the sequence of letters in the printed word... This should be reinforced by teaching them to sound and blend letters in order to pronounce words and to spell words using magnetic letters.'

- In the Solity study:
  - teaching strategies were 'interleaved' throughout the day rather than during an intensive hour;

- lower attaining pupils were taught synthesis skills, segmentation skills, phonic skills and a sight vocabulary;
- 'the goals of teaching, purposes of reading and instructional strategies' were explained and made explicit;
- wide range of books available;
- brought together as a group for two minutes three times a day to review the content of the main teaching sessions, thus the literacy teaching is both structured and systematic and 'overlearning' is built in.

The major literature digest in the area is by Beard (1998). From this extensive study we quote only those points salient to our own work:

- *Success for All* (Slavin, 1996) - main features are essentially as those of the NLS plus 'additional systematic intervention for children at-risk after one year's schooling'.
- *Early Literacy Research Project* (Crevola and Hill, 1998) Melbourne, Australia. Three 'waves' of teaching:
  - 'Good teaching in the first year of school' leads to 80% of pupils having reading and writing 'underway'.
  - Next 20% - Marie Clay's 'Reading Recovery'. Eighteen of the 20% now succeed.
  - Final 2% need 'further referral and special support'.

In our experience the Reading Recovery methods challenge to the pupil's visual memory is such that those with even mild to moderate dyslexia soon stop making progress. Our findings in the development of *A Multi-sensory Teaching for Reading* (Johnson, Phillips and Peer, 1999) and those of Solity et al and Watson (op.cit.) would suggest that, provided during the 'First Wave' there has been effective identification of pupils with dyslexia, then one-to-one teaching from a highly trained specialist may be unnecessary at the Second Wave level. What these pupils need are structured, sequential, synthetic and preferably multi-sensory methods. Given the right materials and some professional development a class teacher supported by an additional adult can effectively teach this group. Where we would emphatically concur is that any pupil not showing a rapid increase in their rate of reading development given this additional intervention should be referred, as a matter of urgency, for specialist assessment and subsequent intensive teaching from an appropriately qualified person.

- *School Matters* (Mortimore et al., 1998) classroom lessons in effective schools included:
  - structured sessions with an 'audit' of tasks achieved,
  - use of 'higher-order questions and statements',
  - sessions with 'limited focus' - one curricular area with differentiation
  - communication between teachers and pupils.
- Harrison (1999): When teachers concentrate their teaching on hearing individual children read, other children may spend up to one-third of their time off-task. (Whilst both Solity et al and Watson and Johnston see individual reading as essential in consolidating developing skills, this would be much more focused 'practice' than the conventional 'reading round the class'.)
- Eldredge, Rentzel and Hollingsworth (1996) found 'shared reading' superior to 'round robin' techniques in matched groups of 7-8 year-olds.
- Beard notes that Holdaway's (1979) early work with Big Books did not involve commercially produced material but transcribed extracts from popular texts on 'newsprint' or overhead transparencies. The proposed increase in the numbers of 'additional adults' to support Literacy Hour teaching may allow a return to this more informal method of producing materials which might have the advantage of enabling a better 'fit' between the materials and the needs of the class.

- HMI Littlewood (Personal Communication, June 1999): 'Good Literacy Hour lessons in Special Schools':
  - Texts need to be well matched to the pupils' understanding.
  - Questions to underpin understanding need to be carefully considered so as not to confuse pupils.
  - Questions to reveal areas of weakness need to be precise and not undermine previously well-learned knowledge.
  - It's important to provide pupils with a greater insight into their problems and strategies to tackle them.
  - Routines which pupils are expected to follow should be practised and demonstrated by the teacher to model the way in which progress can be made.

All of the above points to the need to consider *sequence* of teaching as well as structure, and most importantly, to provide the *personal* messages being given to the pupils. Teaching does not take place in the abstract. The classroom is a social context within which each child develops a concept of him/herself *as a learner*. Structured, sequential teaching means that they begin to feel safe enough to *engage* with learning. It becomes something they can do, not just something that might, one day, happen to them! How a pupil feels about school will affect the degree to which s/he is willing to become involved with reading at all. This is why ultimately if they don't learn from the way we teach, we will have to teach in the way that they learn.

Interviews and observations
The results will be related to the Literacy Hour 'clock' dealing with each part in turn.

Whole class work - shared reading or writing
There was unanimous agreement that this part of the Literacy Hour was beneficial for pupils with SEN in several ways and their inclusion in it caused few problems. Typical comments were that pupils with SEN (including dyslexia) were now better able to concentrate and were more confident and willing to contribute. They were looking more closely at text, and reading together with the other pupils. This 'together' has developed into co-operation and several teachers quoted instances of pupils giving others 'clues' as to the answers to questions.

The Big Books and shared story work was seen as highly motivating. Pupils were reported to be eager on Monday mornings to know what this week's book was. As one child put it, '*I like it when it's the first lesson 'cos it gets you in the mood for work.*' Attention to author, other books in a series or by that author, title, even publisher had previously not been considered or seen as significant - particularly for pupils with SEN. Prior to the Literacy Hour text for pupils with SEN had been kept within the boundaries of their restricted oral reading vocabularies. Whole class work meant that they were now exposed to a much wider and richer one. One teacher was using *Beowulf* as her text at Key Stage 2 in a school in a very deprived area where pupils' spoken language was a problem. She noted the intense interest in words and language that this text, which she would not previously have considered using, aroused in the children. From this developed an enthusiasm for 'playing with language'. Thus, even when the activity would previously have been considered 'beyond them' they gained benefit by joining in the corporate first part, co-operating in other parts and now feeling a part of the whole class rather than apart from it.

However, there was also concern that the structure of the Literacy Hour meant that teachers had little time to consolidate and revise work with pupils with SEN. Whilst there was more reading going on there was a decrease in the amount of time for individual reading. The pupils with SEN were further disadvantaged by their slower decoding skills and they were thus not able to keep up with the class during the shared reading. Focused work on phonics had benefited the generality of children in the class but 'insufficient time to consolidate the work with pupils with SEN' suggests that those needing carefully structured, sequential, probably multi-sensory methods were not getting them.

Strategies for helping pupils with Literacy Difficulties (including dyslexia)

- Teach them the overall structure and the names of the sections.
- Teach them the routine for each section (then stick to it!).
- Identify each section, 'Now we are going to groups for Guided Reading.'
- Think out the *sequence* of teaching points and explain it to pupils.
- Keep the number of new teaching points in each lesson very low.
- Review important prior learning regularly and always link to new teaching.
- Literacy Hour 'Framework' encourages a 'brisk' pace in lessons. Make sure some pupils, particularly those with dyslexic-type difficulties, are not being left behind.
- The speed of progress through the curriculum should allow for 'overlearning'. Pupils need to practise and review essential points until their recall is automatic.
- Review isn't testing - prompt and tell, then ask them to repeat. You want the *right* answer to be what they remember.
- Enhanced self-esteem and confidence are important - but not enough. They need to master the details.
- Use 'open' questions when teaching. 'What do you feel, think, expect etc.?' Accept and mould the pupil's answer.
- Have a 'secret sign' to tell a pupil that the next question will be for him or her.
- Differentiation should be to engage with a task, not just to complete it.
- Co-operation is great - but not if others do all the work.

Whole class work - word/sentence work

Focused work on phonics had benefited the generality of children in the class but teachers also felt that they had 'insufficient time to consolidate the work with pupils with SEN' suggesting those needing carefully structured, sequential, probably multi-sensory methods are not getting them.

However, Cox (1983) says:

'Eighty per cent of all normal children can successfully learn to read by any method of teaching … The remaining 20% who are physically and intellectually normal but who have difficulty in auditory, visual and/or kinaesthetic recognition or memory, must learn all of the language skills through a logically structured, multi-sensory presentation.'

The three studies quoted earlier suggest that this means the use of synthetic rather than analytic phonics.

Analytic phonics

Whole word presentation - child's attention is drawn to letters and sounds within the words - ie analysing the word for sounds.

Synthetic phonics

- Letter sounds are taught and pupils shown how they can build words from independent sounds.
- Pupils learn to form words from sounds as soon as possible.

This is where you may have to depart from the Literacy Hour directions. Whilst not suggesting either analytic or synthetic methods, the *National Literacy Strategy* does see word level work at Key Stage 1 as:

Phonological Awareness - 'Identifying and discriminating sounds in spoken language and recognising their corresponding spelling patterns.'

Word Recognition - 'Identifies a range of words that need to be learned on sight. In the early stages these tend to be high frequency words, which are often irregularly spelt.'

(NLS OHT 1.6)

These methods present challenges to pupils with SEN, particularly those with dyslexia. They need to be directly *taught* grapheme/phoneme correspondences before being expected to identify them. Learning a sight vocabulary will be difficult, if not impossible because of memory problems. Being faced with irregular words before they have confidence that they can confidently decode regular ones can result in pupils regarding reading as something they may never do!

Our earlier work in the development of 'A Multi-sensory Teaching System for Reading' (Johnson, Phillips and Peer, 1999) also showed that introducing, 'Rules which govern written language and the morphemic structure of words (NLS OHT 1.6) not only need not, but should not be delayed until Key Stage 2. Learning the rules that govern over 80% of English can be invaluable to pupils with SEN.'

Teachers can use their professional judgement about how to teach pupils who are not finding learning literacy easy with confidence from Running Records etc. showing significantly better attainments on the part of those pupils.

Group and independent work

Most teachers reported having found the need to teach pupils *how* to work independently, to give them strategies for seeking help from sources other than the teacher if they 'got stuck' and for recognising when and for how long they were to work on their own or with an adult.

Prior to the Literacy Hour pupils with SEN have often been taught *how* to do a task rather than to understand the learning that underlay it. For example, they would have to put words in spaces or boxes from a given list. Now group work must have a common theme for all the class or the pupils with SEN would experience difficulties recognising what they had to do. Similarly, it was important that they complete the Group Word Learning Task even if they did not have to write it down. They must also be helped to prepare to explain what they had done so as to report in the plenary. It was recognised that pupils with SEN needed to learn how to explain what they had done. They must not feel that it was different from that of other groups. In all, there was a much clearer recognition of the emotional side of learning.

A dilemma in relation to previous practice was recognised. Pupils with SEN were formerly given more teacher-time than other pupils. Now an equal amount of time should be spent with each group. Teachers are concerned that without an additional adult they might not now be giving these pupils the attention they need. As one of the teachers said in her interview:

'This is one of our major problems, to be honest. When the *Literacy Strategy* first came in we'd always been spending a lot of time with our least able children, probably more than anyone else, and so the fact that you're spending one 20-minute session each week with them rather than, probably, every day as it was before, we found that really, really difficult. I think we worried that we were just giving them time-filling activities.'

Unfortunately the practice of working with one group each day has resulted in pupils with SEN only receiving the teacher's attention once a week.

Strategies for helping pupils with literacy difficulties (including dyslexia)

- Be very clear about targets, eg 'Write three sentences on ***** before 10.15.'
- Write targets on a sheet of card and prop it up on the table.
- Have another card with 'Group Work Rule Reminders':
  'Have I:
  - joined my writing?
  - co-operated?
  - listened to the teacher?
  - stayed on task?'

(Do not write them on the board. Pupils with dyslexia have great difficulty reading from the chalkboard.)

- Have 'task boards' for those who finish early.
- Have clear classroom roles for broken pencils etc.
- Have self-report checklists for pupil evaluation, eg spelling, punctuation, helpfulness, on-task time.
- Remind them how the time is passing, 'You have five more minutes,' 'Have you done six words yet?'
- Periodically break off and 'flip round' other groups, making sure they are doing the right task.
- Modify games to which pupils already know the rules (eg dominoes) with literacy content.
- Use mixed-ability grouping so groups contain a pupil who can be asked for help.
- Encourage co-operative working in preparation for group responding in the plenary.
- Give praise and reinforcement for specific achievements or behaviours - 'Well done, Jane, you have two good sentences there.' 'Good quiet work, Blue Group, excellent.' Even a quiet smile and a nod or 'thumbs up' after looking at a child's work can enhance attainment.

Work done in whole class work was capitalised on here in that detailed analysis of text taught them how to structure sentences and had increased awareness of vocabulary and language. Comments about 'structure' were recurrent in the interview schedules. The *National Literacy Strategy* had made teachers much more aware that not only were there structures in reading, writing and comprehension but that these structures could be taught. Having learned them, pupils were then better able to read and write fluently.

Pupils with SEN gained in confidence through the Literacy Hour structure. Teachers noted that such pupils now realised that their *ideas* were equal to everyone else's, felt a bigger part of the school day, could contribute because 'literacy is now more about discussion and less about reams of paper.'

Plenary

Some teachers clearly felt a tension here between ensuring that all groups contributed and making the session more than 'show-and-tell'.

- 'The hardest part is to find a common focus.'
- 'Group work must have a common theme or the plenary means nothing to those with SEN.'

104

- 'You have to make sure they've (pupils with SEN) done the (group) work even if they've not written it down.'
- 'It's very hard for the SEN pupils to explain what they've done.'
- 'It's important that SEN pupils don't feel what they have done is different.'

Teachers resolved this tension in different ways. One teacher got round all the groups during group time with the assistance of an additional adult and picked one topic to talk about. Another took a couple of pieces of children's writing and used them for 'critique' in the same way as the Big Book in the whole class work. Another group of teachers had a special SEN session on Fridays where the plenary focus was on what the pupils with SEN had done during the week. It was also noted that pupils with SEN had often 'had enough' by the time the plenary session is due. (It must always be remembered that if a pupil has SEN then they must put considerable extra effort into any achievement, as they must overcome their difficulties in addition to engaging with the work set.) It was also felt that pupils with SEN might benefit more by continuing with more practical activities related to the work done earlier in the Hour. However, they recognised the value of all pupils feeling that their work was of sufficient value to be *actively* considered by the class. (This is very different from 'having your work put on the wall'.)

The plenary session is of real value to pupils with SEN if it becomes truly a *review* of the crucial elements that have been introduced. These can be reiterated in clear and precise language ready for homework or other short review sessions outside the Literacy Hour. They will also be ready for another review at the start of the next day's work.

Conclusion

It is clear from the research that the Literacy Hour has had a major impact on literacy teaching in primary schools. It has generated feelings of success and enthusiasm on the part of both teachers and pupils. Any difficulties seem to relate to the need for *sequencing* as well as structuring work for pupils with SEN (particularly dyslexia). Schools also need to feel more confident that they can diverge from the Framework, particularly with regard to word level work if they can justify the alternative methods and present evidence of more effective learning by pupils.

References

Beard, R. (1998) *National Literacy Strategy: review of Research and other Related Evidence.* London: DfEE.

Cox, A. R. (1985) 'Alphabetic Phonics. An organisation and expansion of Orton-Gillingham'. *Annals of Dyslexia*, 35, 187-198.

DfEE (1999) *Handy Hints for Primary School Teachers.* London: DfEE.

Eldredge, J. L., Reutzel, J. R. and Hollingsworth, P. M. (1996) 'Comparing the Effectiveness of Two Oral Reading Practices: Round-Robin and the Shared Book Experience'. *Journal of Literacy Research*, 28, 2, 201-225.

Harris, A. (Ed) (1998) *The LCP Literacy Resource Files.* Leamington Spa: Language Centre Publications.

Harrison, C. (1999) 'Reading research in the United Kingdom' in Kamil, M. (Ed.) *Handbook of Reading Research.* Hillsdale, N. J.: Lawrence Erlbaum.

HMI (1998) *The National Literacy Project:* A report from the Office of Her Majesty's Chief Inspector of Schools. London: DfEE.

Holdaway, D. (1979) *The Foundations of Literacy.* Sydney: Aston Scolastic.

Johnson, M., Phillips, S. and Peer, L. (1999) *A Multi-sensory Teaching System for Reading.* Manchester: Manchester Metropolitan University.

Littlewood, A. (1999) Points concerning the Presentation of the Literacy Hour in Special Schools, Personal Communication.

McCrory, E., Brunswick, N., Price, C., Frith, C. D. and Frith, U. (1999) Dyslexia: What happens later in development? Paper presented to BPS Developmental Psychology Section Annual Conference.

Mortimore, P., Sammons, P., Stoll, L., Lewis, D. and Ecob, R. (1998) *School Matters: The Junior Years*. Wells: Open Books.

Solity, J., Deaves, R., Kerfoot, S., Crane, G. and Cannon, K. (1999) *Early Reading Research: An Overview*. DECP Newsletter 91, June 1999.

Times Educational Supplement, October 1998, p.6 'Literacy Hour is "too long"'.

Times Educational Supplement, November 1998, p.8 'Scots throw down literacy gauntlet'.

Watson, J. E. and Johnston, R. S. (1998) *Accelerating Reading Attainment: The effectiveness of synthetic phonics*. Interchange 57, Edinburgh, The Scottish Office.

©Mike Johnson, Manchester Metropolitan University, Didsbury
Lindsay Peer, British Dyslexia Association

Note: Whilst the work referred to above was commissioned and financed by the DfEE the opinions expressed in this report are the writers' own and do not necessarily reflect those of the DfEE.

Conclusion

Since the *National Literacy Strategy*'s Framework for Teaching was published and its additional guidance, which included advice for teaching children with special educational needs, the DfEE has produced more information and material for use with pupils which can be used for those with learning difficulties. However, the material is not primarily for children with special educational needs.

Additional Literacy Support

The first of these was the Additional Literacy Support (ALS) programme. This is a teaching package for use with those pupils who have not been taught within the Literacy Hour throughout their time in the primary sector. It is designed for pupils in Years 3 and 4 who achieved Level 1 or 2c in the Key Stage 1 SATs, although it is acknowledged that it would also be appropriate for some pupils in Year 5, and is intended to enable these pupils to achieve Level 4 in English at the end of their primary education. LEAs are funded for ALS through the Standards Fund through a formula based on the attainments of pupils in the Key Stage 1 tests. This money is to support extra learning support assistant hours to deliver the programme. A training course over two days would also be delivered.

The programme consists of four teaching module books covering phonics, reading and writing. It is delivered for three sessions a week by the learning support assistant and by the class teacher for one session and each session takes 20 minutes fitting into the group word level session of the Literacy Hour. It is designed to take 24 weeks in total and three modules need to be covered (either Modules 1-3 or 2-4). The training programme is detailed as is the teaching programme.

It is in its infancy but it appears that schools who have started using the materials are finding them well structured and easy to use. Pupils are responding well to the programme but it is too early to give any measured results.

Phonics. Progression in phonics: materials for whole-class teaching

The second set of material which was delivered to schools in November 1999 is a teaching/activity book entitled *Phonics. Progression in phonics: materials for whole-class teaching*. This reinforces what was written about the acquisition of reading in the original Framework (the reading searchlights model) and also augments what was stated in this about the teaching of phonics. It then outlines the progression in the teaching and learning of phonics in seven steps which are linked to the objectives in the original Framework. It is intended for pupils in the early years with the first two stages or steps outlining activities for nursery and young Reception children. These first steps are early phonological awareness games and activities whilst Steps 2-7 divide the learning objectives and the activities into three sections:

- hearing and saying
- identifying phonemes and spelling
- recognising letters and reading.

There are a range of games and activities suggested and the book contains material for use in the sessions. These are designed for use in the 15-minute phonic section of the Literacy Hour and there are three types of activities; those that the adult demonstrates or models; those which involve the children answering called 'show me'; and those where the children are expected to respond actively ('get up and go').

This programme of work has been designed for whole class work rather than group work and the teachers' information states 'experience has shown that even where there are differences in children's ability most children learn from them'. Teachers are sure to evaluate these materials in order to see how they work with pupils with special educational needs and it will be interesting in the future to hear their views.

It is pleasing that the DfEE is producing structured guidance and even materials for use in schools. Maybe there is a lot more to come. It is hoped that practitioners will be invited to evaluate this and to help in future production of materials.

The future

Success in the Literacy Hour shows how much teachers care about those pupils who have learning difficulties, sensory and physical problems, language and social communication problems, and difficulties in controlling their behaviours. With little guidance these teachers are adapting the Literacy Hour to meet their pupils' needs. They are expending energy in making materials. What they are asking for is time and additional adult support so that the Hour can be accessed by all pupils. They should be granted their requests. They need recognition for their patience, their adaptability, their commitment. It is important that their voices are heard and acted upon.

Schools and respondents
Secondary sector
Fakenham High School, Fakenham, Norfolk (Elaine Nickolls)
Hodgson High School Technology College, Poulton-le-Fylde, Lancashire (Lindsey Wilde)
John Bentley School, Calne, Wiltshire (Patricia Wilde)
Tewkesbury School, Tewkesbury, Gloucestershire (Sue Webb)
Ysgol Gyfim Y Cymer, Rhondda (Tim Leyshon)
(One respondent wished to remain anonymous.)

Primary/middle sector
Ballifield Primary School, Sheffield (C. Waterhouse)
Bell Lane Primary, Hendon, London (Susy Stone)
Coppice Primary School, Four Oaks, London (Fiona Goodwin)
Fairmeadows Foundation Primary School, Swadlincote, Derbyshire (Elaine Day)
Front Lawn Junior, Havant, Hampshire (Sharon Merrick)
Greenway School, Horsham, West Sussex (J. Malsbury)
Moat Farm Infants, Oldbury, West Midlands (Janet Spencer)
Morecambe Road School, Morecambe, Lancashire (G. Cunningham)
Ocklynge Junior School, Eastbourne (P. Westwood)
Pakefield Middle School, Lowestoft, Suffolk (Lynda Steer)
Portland Primary School, Birkenhead, Wirral (J. Hart)
Roydon CP School, Diss, Norfolk (F. Jones)
St. Mary's CEVAP, Woodbridge, Suffolk (Alison Davis)
Towerbank Primary, Edinburgh, Scotland (A. Morrison)
Treetops School, Grays, Essex (Mick Simmonds)

Contributors names only
E. Black, Scotland
N. Desalro
Elvie Herd, Luton
J. M. Craven
(A few contributors wished to remain anonymous.)

Special schools
Alderman Kay Special School, Middleton (Elaine Dutton)
Battledown Children's Centre, Cheltenham, Gloucester (Siân Bailey)
Conductive Education Centre, London (Claire Hewitt)
Freemantles School, Chertsey, Surrey (Jane Vaughan)
Gorse Bank School, Oldham (Bridget Nolan)
Houdsfield Language Unit, Edmonton (L. Mansbridge)
John Watson School, Wheatley, Oxfordshire (Anne Brown and Maeve Lawler)
Pathfield School, Barnstaple, Devon (Claire May)
St. Giles School, Derby, Derbyshire (Jill Moore)
Wood Acre School, South Ockendon, Essex (Jennifer Bailey)

Contributors names only
Steve Rogers, Birmingham
Mandy Townsend, Littlemore, Oxfordshire
(One contributor wished to remain anonymous.)